D1882273

EVEREST:
THE CHALLENGE

Chitral
Hunza
Gilgit
K2
Shaksgam
Baltoro
Nanga Parbat
KASHMIR
Srinagar
R. Indus
English Miles
0 50 100 200 300
TIBET
PUNJAB
R. Sutlej
Simla
Kamet
Kailas
Nanda Devi
Ranikhet
Almora
Delhi
R. Brahmaputra
Lhasa
NEPAL
Everest
Kangchenjunga
BHUTAN
Darjiling
R. Ganga
R. Ganges
Benares
Karachi
Ahmadabad
CALCUTTA
Arabian
Bombay
Bay of

EVEREST:
THE CHALLENGE

BY

SIR FRANCIS YOUNGHUSBAND

Illustrated
Second Edition

With a Special Account of the 1936 Expedition

Sir Francis Younghusband has written for this edition an entirely new account of the 1936 attempt on Everest, with a detailed discussion of the problems which the Expedition had to face

GYAN

Published by

Gyan Publishing House
5, Ansari Road
Daryaganj, New Delhi-110002
Phone: 011-47034999, 9811692060
E-mail: books@gyanbooks.com

Distribution Network
gyanbooks.com
India, USA, Canada, UK, Australia, France

© **Publisher**
All rights reserved. No part of this work may be reproduced, stored, adapted, or transmitted in any form or by any means, electronic, mechanical, photocopying, micro-filming, recording or otherwise, or translated in any language, without the prior written permission of the copyright owner and the publisher.

ISBN : 978-81-212-2923-4 (PB)
First Published, 1936

2nd Impression 2021

Printed at: Gyan Press, Delhi.

The book is sold subject to the condition that it shall not, by way of trade or otherwise, be lent, resold, hired out, or otherwise circulated without the prior publisher's written consent.

Everest: The Challenge
Author: Sir Francis Younghusband

EVEREST: THE CHALLENGE

by

SIR FRANCIS YOUNGHUSBAND

Illustrated

Second Edition

With a Special Account of the 1936 Expedition

Sir Francis Younghusband has written for this edition an entirely new account of the 1936 attempt on Everest, with a detailed discussion of the problems which the Expedition had to face

THOMAS NELSON AND SONS LTD
LONDON EDINBURGH PARIS MELBOURNE
TORONTO AND NEW YORK

Photograph by A. F. R. Wollaston.

EVEREST FROM THE NORTH-EAST.

PREFACE

This book was conceived and half written before I knew that another Everest Expedition was to be dispatched. When I retired from the Mount Everest Committee in 1934 I thought that, owing to the death of the Dalai Lama, permission for another expedition would not be granted by the Tibetans for many years. The news that permission had been given came therefore as a complete surprise. As far as this book is concerned the news was also most welcome; for an Everest Expedition will fulfil the main purpose of the book, which is to attract the attention of the world to the Himalaya. And the attention of men needs to be drawn thither, for in those mountains untold wealth is to be found.

But here at the start I must say one word on how to pronounce the name of this region. I ought to be able to pronounce the name of the mountains in which I was born, but I doubt if I can. Himalaya is the short for Himál-láya, snow-abode. And Indians pronounce it in a flowing rhythmic way without any very decided accent on either of the first two a's.

In telling the story of the various expeditions I am deeply indebted to Ruttledge's great book, *Everest: 1933*, to Smythe's *Conquest of Kamet*, and to the descriptions of the German Expeditions to Kangchenjunga and Nanga Parbat, and of Oliver's, Shipton's, and Marco Pallis's Expeditions to the Kumaon Himalaya in the *Alpine Journal*. My own part has been chiefly to indicate the connection between these various efforts, and to show how all are directly the result of the challenge which Everest offers to men to come and climb the Himalaya.

I have a hatred of all photographs of the Himalaya. They degrade the mountains in the minds of all who have seen them. But in the eyes of those who have not seen them, photographs are supposed to give some slight impression of what the mountains are like, so I reluctantly comply with my publisher's request to include some. And I offer my warm thanks to the Mount Everest Committee of the Royal Geographical Society and the Alpine Club, Professor Kenneth Mason, H.R.H. the Duke of Spoleto, Mr. Bentley Beetham, the Everest Flight, Mr. F. S. Smythe, and Mr. John Murray for the use of their photographs.

F. Y.

February 1936.

CONTENTS

Book I: Adventure

Book II: Reflection

ILLUSTRATIONS

MAPS AND DIAGRAMS

EVEREST: THE CHALLENGE

CHAPTER I

THE INCEPTION OF THE IDEA

HOW exactly the idea of climbing the highest mountain in the world arose in the mind of man is difficult to trace. All we can say is that many contributory influences went to the creation of it. There was no one individual who stood up and said: "I mean to get to the top of Everest." First one man's mind would move in that direction. This, long after, would stir another. He would influence a third, and so on. It was only by slow degrees and over many years that man made up his mind and braced his will to climb the highest mountain.

For that is a staggering adventure. To any ordinary individual who first saw Mont Blanc the thought would never occur that a man would dare to reach its summit. And even when we know that hundreds of persons every year accomplish that feat we do not, on first seeing a Himalayan giant, presume to think that man could ever stand upon its summit. Certainly, the idea never entered my mind as I first travelled amongst the greater Himalayan peaks in 1887. Two years before, I had spoken with an officer of the Survey of India about Graham's reported ascent to about 24,000 feet on Kabru, and he had assured me that Graham must have mistaken his peak, for no man could climb so high: 22,000 feet was the limit. And this was the accepted idea fifty years ago. The highest peak of the Himalaya must for ever lie outside the range of human capacity.

When, two years later, in 1887, I came right alongside some of the supreme peaks, I was confirmed in this belief. As I saw them at close quarters, I realized the absurdity of supposing that men could reach their summits.

I was exploring a route across the Himalaya by an unknown pass. Each turn had its surprises. And one turn had the most astounding surprise. As I was ascending the valley which led up to the Mustagh Pass, and had rounded the end of a spur, there suddenly came into view a sight which brought me to an immediate standstill, and made me gasp with amazement. It was a mountain unbelievably higher than anything I had imagined, and I was only a few miles from its base, so that I could realize its height to the full.

I knew not what mountain it was; but I found afterwards that it was no other than K_2, the second highest mountain in the world, 28,250 feet in altitude, and only 750 feet lower than Everest itself.

The sight of it was a thrilling experience for a young man to have. As a boy I had been excited by the first sight of the Alps. They were great enough. But this was greater far. I cannot remember having been struck with my own insignificance in comparison with this giant of a mountain. My dominant feeling was one of delight—of joy at having had the chance of seeing so wonderful a sight. And on that occasion, as well as two years later, when I traversed that marvellous region round K_2, and, from close under them, saw its satellites of 27,000 feet, 26,000 feet, and 25,000 feet peaks, I feasted my soul on their beauty. But, full of spirit as I was, the idea that I, or any one else, should presume to think of climbing any one of them never entered my mind. I believed myself adventurous, but adventurous to that extent I decidedly was not. My spirit was still at the pass level. It had risen above the valleys. But most certainly it had not risen to the peaks. When, therefore, I looked upon these giants round me, I just took it for granted that their summits were for ever beyond the reach of man.

The first to elevate my spirit above the placid pass level was Martin Conway. On my return from my journeys in this region, and on the Pamirs in 1891, he asked me if I could tell him of some fairly accessible peak of 25,000 feet. The first I thought of was Mustagh Ata on the Pamirs, which seemed to have a fairly accessible slope to the summit. And next to it I thought of that most beautiful mountain, Rakapushi, in Hunza. As every one knows, Conway, with Bruce and others, explored and surveyed the Baltoro region round K_2, and made an attempt to ascend Rakapushi. He was not successful in climbing to anywhere near the 25,000-feet level. But he did set the mind of man towards attaining the supreme heights ; and man has fastened on them ever since.

Following him came Mummery, that most trained and skilled and joyous of all great climbers. His ambition rose higher than 25,000 feet. He would pit himself against Nanga Parbat, that superb mountain which rises to a height of 26,620 feet, and in solitary glory dominates all the region round—the monarch of Kashmir. What became of him no one knows. He was probably swept away in an avalanche, and not a sign of him has ever appeared again.

Nothing daunted, man still pressed his attack. Expedition after expedition came out to the Himalaya. Longstaff climbed Trisul, 23,406 feet in height. The Bullock-Workmans climbed to nearly that height.

Man's spirit was now mounting. He even began to aspire to the highest. He would not acknowledge it openly. But he nourished the great ambition in his secret heart. The Duke of the Abruzzi, with the most perfectly organized expedition that had then come out to the Himalaya, arrived in Kashmir in the summer of 1909. Publicly it was " a mountaineering and exploring expedition which proposed as its aim the investigation of the problem concerning the possibility of ascending the highest peaks." Privately, and in less stilted language, it was an effort to climb K_2. And K_2 had only been chosen because access to Everest was closed by the seclusive policy of the Nepalese Govern-

Photograph by the Duke of Spoleto's Expedition.

K_2 FROM THE NORTH.

ment on the south, and the Tibetan Government on the north. If either of these two governments had been favourable, the Duke would not have spent so much energy in trying to climb K_2.

The Duke of the Abruzzi was himself an ideal leader of such enterprise. He had already led successful mountaineering expeditions to Ruwenzori in Central Africa, and Mount St. Elias in Alaska. He was about thirty-six years of age, slim and wiry of body, burning with the most ardent spirit, a natural leader of men, European or Asiatic, and a most efficient organizer. No worthier foeman has matched himself against the Himalayan giants. And he brought with him besides the experienced scientist and mountaineer, Dr. de Filippi, and the finest of all mountain photographers, Vittorio Sella, four Italian guides, and four Italian porters.

It was a strange coincidence that they set out on their quest of K_2—and, they secretly hoped, conquest—from my house in Kashmir. What I had never imagined to be within the bounds of possibility when I first saw the mountain twenty-two years before, they were now to put to test.

Dr. de Filippi has given us the impression which this remote region round K_2 made upon them. The scale was too vast, he says, for one to receive at once an impression of the whole. The eye could only take in single portions. For a long time they did not become fully conscious of the dimensions of the landscape. They had no standard of comparison. The glaciers and valleys were so well adjusted in their proportions to the surrounding mountains that it was hard to realize the true size of any object. They would repeatedly fail in estimating heights and distances. They were in a world built upon proportions so incomparably larger than those of the familiar Alps that the judgment of even the most expert among them was found wanting.

Immense chains rose all about them as far as the eye could see. And, in spite of their size, the mountains had all the bold design to be seen anywhere in the Alps—the barren precipices, the snowy slopes, the upward thrust of slender peaks. There was the richest variety of design, the greatest majesty of form, and an infinite variety of plane and perspective. But all this was there with such luxuriance, and upon such a gigantic scale, that they stood bewildered in the midst of a scene that beggared human imagination. So inconceivably vast were the structural lines of the landscape that they seemed to be in Nature's workshop, standing before the primeval chaos while the world was still unvisited by the phenomena of life.

And this impression, so strong and moving, did not diminish with familiarity. Their amazement grew greater every day. This extraordinary region never made a profounder impression on them than on the day when they bade it farewell.

This is the testimony of one whose native country is bounded by the Alps, and who was thoroughly familiar with them. It is especially valuable as showing how different is the scale on which the Himalaya is built.

The goal of their ambition was not, however, to be seen till many days after they had entered this Baltoro region. It was hidden away at the far end. As they neared it they were seized with unspeakable restlessness, fearing lest mist should cut them off from the long-looked-for reward of their efforts. Suddenly, at the end of a glacier, they saw K_2, the " indisputable monarch of this region, gigantic and solitary, hidden from human sight by innumerable ranges, jealously defended by a vast throng of vassal peaks, protected from invasion by miles and miles of glacier."

The mountain filled the whole end of the valley, with nothing to draw the attention from it. Its lines were ideally proportioned and perfectly balanced, and its powerful architectural design was adequate to its majesty without being heavy. But the steepness of its sides, and its glaciers, were appalling. Its rocky wall was 12,000 feet in height. And as the Duke and his companions gazed at it, minutely inspected and examined it with their glasses, their minds were assailed with increasing doubts as to its accessibility. There did not appear to be a single point at which it could reasonably be attacked.

However, the Duke decided to make at least an attempt upon it by the southern ridge. Almost everywhere on this ridge they could see with their binoculars the gleam of bare ice, hard and polished like crystal. Still, a few days' sun might clear them, and preparations were made to send up a small camp on to the ridge, and the Duke set out with three Italian guides, four Italian porters, and some Balti coolies. But the effort was of no avail. They had not reached higher than 20,000 feet when the guides came to the reluctant conclusion that it was useless to proceed farther, not so much because of any insuperable obstacles which they themselves had so far encountered, as because there was no likelihood of coolies being able to carry loads for the several camps which would be required in so long an ascent. K_2 could not be climbed in one long day as a Swiss mountain might be climbed. Successive camps would have to be established upon it in which the climbers would be able to spend the nights. And the guides saw no possibility of this being done with the men at their disposal. After examining the mountain from all sides, they finally came to the conclusion that K_2 was not to be climbed.

The Duke did not, however, give up the idea of ascending some lesser peak. He still wished to test how high a man could climb. He therefore selected a comparatively easy peak—Bride Peak, 25,110 feet. And he might very well have reached the summit had not mist prevented his reaching a higher altitude than 24,600 feet.

This, for many years, stood as the record of achievement in altitude. And the fact that the Duke and his guides had lived for seventeen days never below 18,000 feet, and on nine of these above 21,000 feet, and made one ascent to 23,458 feet and another to 24,600 feet, gave encouragement to the hopes that some day still higher heights might be reached.

This was a most valuable result of this carefully planned expedition. It showed how the spirit of man was rising. In 1892 Conway had still doubted whether it would be possible to reach the 24,000-feet level. The Bullock-Workmans had thought it would be impossible to sleep properly and protect oneself from cold at over 21,000 feet. But now Dr. de Filippi concluded that " altitude is not to be considered as in itself an obstacle to an ascent." . . . " The progressive history of mountain climbing, from its inception down to the present day, seems to show that man's power of endurance and capacity of exertion at great heights have steadily increased."

This was the attitude of mind among mountaineers in the years preceding the Great War. Lord Curzon, when Viceroy of India, had suggested to Douglas Freshfield, then President of the Alpine Club, the dispatch of an expedition to Mount Everest through Nepal, if the permission of the Nepalese Government could be obtained. But this was not obtainable, and, in any case, there was then no very serious intention of climbing the mountain to its summit. Reaching the mountain was about as much as was then thought of—reconnoitring its approaches as Freshfield had reconnoitred Kangchenjunga.

The idea of actually climbing the mountain only took precise shape after the Great War. Then at last we came to the point when man did quite definitely make up his mind to climb the highest mountain in the world—when the indecisive urges of the past settled into the one direction, and the will determined to carry out what the mind had decided.

The moment came at a meeting of the Royal Geographical Society in London ; and the man who spoke the decisive thought was the President of the Alpine Club. Captain J. B. Noel was delivering a lecture on a surreptitious reconnaissance towards Everest which he had made before the war. In it he made no reference to anything more than approaching the mountain : he made no suggestion of attempting to reach its summit. But in the discussion which followed the delivery of the lecture, Captain Percy Farrar, who was then President of the Alpine Club, made the decisive leap forward. He spoke of the summit itself. He said that the Alpine Club naturally viewed with the keenest interest the proposal to attempt the ascent of Mount Everest. Moreover, it seemed to him that the attempt now commanded chances of success not previously available. The Alpine Club was prepared not only to lend such financial aid as was in its power, but also to recommend two or three young mountaineers quite capable of dealing with any purely mountaineering difficulties that were likely to be met with.

This was the spark which set flame to the train. I was sitting by Farrar as he spoke. When he finished, I asked the President of the Geographical Society to let me say a few words, though the evening was already late. I said it was now twenty-six years since Captain Bruce had made the proposition to me that we should "go up Mount Everest." Our own Society was interested in the project. We had heard the President of the Alpine Club say that he had magnificent young mountaineers ready to undertake it. And it must be done, I said, though there might be one or two attempts before we were successful. The first thing we would have to do would be to get over trouble with our own Government. But, after all, Government would be reasonable if they were approached properly and by Societies like ours and the Alpine Club. I finished by saying that this was a big business, and must be done in a big way, and I hoped something really serious would come of the meeting.

I had a talk with Farrar afterwards. He said the men he had in mind were the brothers Finch, but there were other capable young climbers who would be available; and he was all in favour of an attempt being made.

Now it so happened that I myself was about to succeed to the Presidency of the Royal Geographical Society, and I determined to make this Everest venture the main feature of my three years' Presidency. With my special knowledge both of the Tibetan Government and of the Government of India, and also of its supervising authority, the India Office in London, I thought I would be in a peculiarly good position for initiating such an enterprise; and with the President of the Alpine Club so ready to help it forward the chances of success were greatly increased. So when I became President I formed a Mount Everest Committee of representatives of the Society and the Club.

Theoretically it would have been better for some private individual to have come forward to initiate and conduct his own expedition as Bruce, Longstaff, and Mumm had attacked Trisul. And the method of running Everest expeditions by Committee has been severely criticized by R. G. Irving in his recent book, *The Romance of Mountaineering*. Mr. Irving is the Winchester master who first inspired the Winchester boy, Mallory, to mountaineer. And he voices the views of many mountaineers when he objects to the system of selecting climbers—selecting them instead of waiting for them to initiate a climb. The Everest expeditions are not, he contends, the result of individual enterprise. The selection of the climbers and the payment of the cost are the responsibility of men of whom few have taken part in the actual climbing of the mountain. So, however much the selectors may endeavour to impress upon the men picked for the struggle the need of caution, they cannot relieve them entirely of the feeling that they were being selected and sent out to accomplish a particular feat ; and failure to accomplish that feat will bring disappointment to others besides themselves. Moreover, mountaineering is suffering from the publicity accorded to other sports and arts. " By all means let us encourage men to go on their own responsibility to climb the Himalaya and any other mountain, but do not let us set the ring for them as we have begun to do. Our great footballers, our great cricketers have become public entertainers, and we must accept the fact. Mountaineering is altogether unfitted to follow such a trend."

Much else Mr. Irving writes in criticism of the initiators of the Everest expeditions. And we may readily admit that there would be more of the romance of mountaineering if some enterprising individual got together some fellow-mountaineers, collected the necessary funds, and set off to conquer Everest. The Duke of Abruzzi organized such a party to conquer one of the giants of the Karakoram Himalaya. Mummery led such a party to climb Nanga Parbat. Undoubtedly it is a far better method when the object of the expedition is any other mountain than Mount Everest.

But for climbing Mount Everest another method is necessary. Everest is not easily accessible. It is situated in the most seclusive country in the world. The Tibetans like to keep themselves to themselves. They dislike foreigners entering their country. And this feeling was so far respected by the British Government that even after the Mission to Lhasa of 1904, the India Office in London were unwilling to ask permission from the Tibetan Government for travellers to enter Tibet: the argument being that a British traveller in Tibet might be the cause of trouble with the Tibetans, possibly leading to intervention—why then run the risk? Why not let sleeping dogs lie? The prospect of a private individual with a band of fellow-mountaineers getting past even the India Office was remote. But what the India Office and the Tibetan Government might not do for private irresponsible individuals they might conceivably do for responsible bodies like the Royal Geographical Society and the Alpine Club. Approached by Presidents of these two august and influential Societies even the most cautious Secretary of State for India might be disposed to relax. This, then, was one reason why an Everest Committee was formed.

Another reason was that not one, but at least two, and probably a series of expeditions would have to be dispatched before the summit was finally reached. When these expeditions were first inaugurated practically nothing was known about the mountain except its height and its latitude and longitude. No European had been within forty miles of it. We knew nothing of its immediate approaches. One expedition would therefore have to be occupied with the preliminary work of reconnaissance. And though we hoped that the second expedition might attain the summit, we had to expect that a third might be necessary. Evidently there must be steady continuity of effort over a number of years, and this was another reason for forming a Committee instead of awaiting sporadic efforts of separate individuals.

Ideally, it would have been delightful if a band of happy mountaineers, accustomed to climbing together on holidays in the Alps, would have undertaken the tremendous task of tackling Everest. But in practice this was not feasible. At any rate, no such band came forward. And even if it had, the probability is that it would have been incapable of giving to the enterprise that sustained continuity of effort which the Committee of a permanent Society can provide.

Thus it came about that the attack on Mount Everest was organized by a Committee and not by an individual.

But others besides Mr. Irving looked askance at the venture. It was merely spectacular and sensational, thought some. Not scientific—not the kind of thing to be deliberately encouraged by a serious body like the Royal Geographical Society. Others of a less scientific but more poetic frame of mind thought it a shame to break into the mystery of the mountain. How much better it would be to leave the mountain in her splendour unsullied by the foot of man ! But the Everest Committee were nakedly and unashamedly bent upon helping man to place his foot on the summit of Everest. Science would gain by knowing how that could be done. And poetry certainly would not lose ; for what more glorious theme for a poem could there be found than this epic of man's struggle with the mountain—of his proving his own powers against the powers of the mountain, testing them to the utmost and unknown stretch of their capacity against the likewise unknown powers of the mountain—slaying no one, hurting no one, but ready to endure severest cold and the fiercest blizzards, to risk dangers from avalanches and icy slopes, and to sacrifice all in order that others might go forward!

So the great adventure was launched. Through the instrumentality of Colonel Howard-Bury, who volunteered to go out to India for the purpose, the support of the Government of India was obtained; and through the tact of Sir Charles Bell, the consent of the Tibetan Government. It then only remained to raise the money and choose the personnel, and man embarked on the definite enterprise of scaling the supreme summit of this world. Whether that was within or outside his capacities he knew not. At any rate, he would have a try. He would not sit still merely gazing at the summit.

Chapter II

THE ATTEMPT

WE had obtained the necessary permission from the Tibetan Government; we had raised the necessary funds; we had got together a body of climbers; but the prime object of the first expedition sent out to Tibet was not to climb the mountain: it was to reconnoitre the approaches and prospect a likely way up. For when this first expedition was dispatched to Everest practically nothing was known about the mountain except that it was 29,002 feet above sea-level, and that, from a distance, the upper part looked as if it might be climbed. There appeared to be a long, even slope towards the summit: it did not seem to be so utterly inaccessible as, for example, the summit of K_2. But no one had been within forty miles of the mountain, and, for all we then knew, it might be quite impossible to climb up on to that sloping ridge which seemed to lead so conveniently to the summit. Further, that ridge itself, easy though it might appear from a distance, might, at close quarters, present many an impassable obstacle.

The first expedition was, therefore, sent out with the special object of reconnoitring the mountain, finding out the best approach, and determining the best line of attack—though the members were not precluded from making an attempt to reach the summit should a favourable opportunity occur. Those were days of great innocence. I cannot remember the graver mountaineers, like Meade and Longstaff, who had both climbed to 23,000 feet, ever giving countenance to so wild a suggestion, but the more childlike optimists, like Farrar and myself, indulged in the dream that *perhaps,* after all, the mountain might not be so very difficult, the lack of oxygen in the air might not be so serious an obstacle, there might be no insuperable hindrance to a great climber like Mallory reaching the top. It was not probable, but it was possible. Mont Blanc, which had so distressed its first climbers, was thought nothing of now. It might be the same with Everest. There was, anyhow, a bare possibility that it might be climbed. And the more sanguine of us in our more sanguine moods hugged that possibility.

How very bare that possibility was the reports from the reconnaissance party soon, however, showed us. Howard-Bury who, on account of his previous experience in India and in the Himalaya, had been placed in charge of the expedition, had dispatched Mallory up the huge glacier which flows from the north face of Everest. He named it the Rongbuk Glacier, after the monastery near its mouth. And Mallory ascended it to near its source. But there he was confronted by the most forbidding, utterly unclimbable cliffs. Above was that comparatively easy-looking ridge leading to the summit. There was, however, no means from this direction of getting on to the ridge. Only one chink there was in this terriffic defence—a gap, afterwards called the North Col. Mallory could see this from the head of the Rongbuk, but could not reach it. He rightly surmised, however, that it might be reached from the opposite direction. The whole expedition, therefore, moved round the mountain, and Everest was reconnoitred from the east. By a piece of fine mountaineering Mallory succeeded in climbing up the ice-fall on to the North Col, 23,000 feet. From there he looked up the great north face of Everest. " For a long way up those easy rock and snow slopes was neither danger nor difficulty," he wrote ; " but at present there was wind. And higher was a more fearful sight. The powdery fresh snow on the great face of Everest was being swept along in unbroken spindrift, and the very ridge where our route was marked out had to receive its unmitigated fury."

He had to return, for he was only on a reconnaissance. But the object of the expedition had been attained. He had found a way to the summit—the way that all other expeditions have followed.

The next expedition—this time under that veteran Himalayan mountaineer, General Bruce—set out with the specific purpose of climbing Everest. Bruce himself, on account of his age, would not make the attempt : his rôle was to direct operations as a whole, to organize the expedition, and, in especial, to collect local porters and infuse them with an esprit-de-corps. For the actual climb such magnificent climbers as Mallory, Norton, Somervell, and George Finch were available—and all of them were in the very zenith of their powers.

One great question had, though, to be decided before the expedition started. Should the climbers use oxygen or not? The main obstacle in the way of reaching the summit was the deficiency of oxygen in the air at those extreme altitudes. The physical obstacles on the face of the mountain were not insuperable. The cold might be great: but that again would not prevent men from reaching the summit. The one real obstacle was the oxygen deficiency. Supply that deficiency and the top would be reached.

But to supply the deficiency a heavy and bulky apparatus would be needed. The oxygen would have to be carried under great pressure so as to have a large amount of it in a small space. And for oxygen under high pressure strong metal cylinders would be needed. These would be of some weight—and the apparatus did, in fact, weigh thirty pounds. The question naturally arose, therefore, whether the advantage to be gained by inhaling the oxygen would or would not outweigh the disadvantage of carrying so heavy an apparatus. As two scientific men among the climbers, Somervell and Finch, were strongly in favour of using oxygen, it was decided to equip the expedition with oxygen apparatus. And Finch, who was himself a lecturer in chemistry, as well as a magnificent mountaineer, enthusiastically undertook charge of the oxygenists. I confess that when I saw and lifted the complete oxygen

Photograph by Bentley Beetham.

EVEREST FROM THE BASE CAMP,
showing the streamer of snow from the peak.

outfit for a climber I was aghast at the idea of any one being saddled with such a load. But if the men who would have to be carrying it were not deterred it was not for me to raise objection. So the expedition—with Finch so keen upon using the apparatus that he would like to have had the whole expedition accustoming themselves to it for some hours every day on the voyage out—started in high hopes of reaching the summit.

At the end of March 1922 the expedition left Darjiling, and an incident of note took place at the start. The chief Lamas and Brahmins of the district blessed the party and offered up prayers for its well-being. Similarly, on their arrival at the Rongbuk Monastery, near the foot of Mount Everest, Bruce took his men to be blessed by the Lama, a dignified old gentleman with an extraordinarily attractive smile. The Himalayan porters set great store by these blessings. The very fact that the most spiritual men are ready to give their blessing confirms the porters in their conviction that the enterprise upon which they are about to embark and which will involve them in much danger, is a worthy enterprise. And being convinced on that point, and bearing with them the good wishes of those whom they respect most, they could put their whole hearts unreservedly into the adventure.

The expedition was started with great expectations, but the result was disappointing. We had not learned either the proper use of oxygen or the value of slow acclimatization. The climbers using oxygen were encumbered with far too heavy an apparatus. And the climbers without oxygen were insufficiently acclimatized for the mighty effort required of them. Consequently, neither oxygenists nor non-oxygenists reached even the 28,000-feet level. The first reached an altitude of 27,235 feet, and the latter an altitude of 26,985 feet. This latter was, it is true, 2,300 feet higher than men had ever climbed before. But it might have been exceeded, and would have been exceeded, if Mallory and Norton, the two who made this record, had been better acclimatized on the one hand and less physically exhausted on the other.

Every expedition, whether to the Poles or to Everest, sets out with the idea of keeping the best men in clover to make the final supreme effort. The man or men who are to reach the Pole or the summit are to be saved all unnecessary wear or tear till the last moment, and then launched on the final spring. The rest are to work themselves to the bone. These are to be kept in reserve and at their fittest. Seldom can this theory be carried out in practice. Nearly always there are calls for the best long before the goal is approached. Certainly it was so in this case. Probably no finer climbers than Mallory and Norton will ever attack Everest ; and if only they could have been kept in reserve, quietly acclimatizing themselves without having their physique exhausted by cold, material discomforts, and hard work, they might well have reached the summit even on this first attempt. What prevented this was the obstacle presented by the North Col, 23,000 feet above sea-level. The ascent to this saddle from the head of the glacier

NORTON AND MALLORY AT 27,000 FEET.

which flows away from it, is the stiffest and most dangerous part of the whole way to the summit. It is nothing but an ice-fall of about 1,200 feet, seamed with crevasses and liable to avalanches. The very best men in the party had to be used for tackling it.

Another difficulty was that they were unable to pitch their final camp anywhere near close enough to the summit. At that time it was not known what porters could do. Up till then even unladen men had reached only 24,600 feet above sea-level, and it could hardly be believed that porters carrying twenty-pound loads could climb any higher. Even if they could, there was difficulty on the steep face of Everest in finding an area six feet square on which to pitch a tent. As a result, the spot from which the climbers set out to make the attempt on the summit was not much over 25,000 feet above sea-level, leaving the climbers nearly 4,000 feet to ascend. And this proved too much for them. By 2.30 p.m. they had reached an altitude of only 26,985 feet, and were making a rise of only 400 feet. Possibly they might have reached the summit if they had gone on—but not in time to return before sunset.

The expedition failed to reach the summit, but it achieved one important result. It showed that men can acclimatize themselves to high altitudes. Before this expedition set out it was not known whether climbers would become more capable or less capable of climbing by staying above the 21,000-feet level. We were told that a man would not be able to sleep at 23,000 feet, and that on the second day which he spent at that altitude he would be worse than on the first, and on the third day he would be worse than on the second. The contrary was proved to be the case. A man was better on the second day than on the first, and better on the third than on the second. It was discovered that the human organism could adapt itself to the new conditions. The lungs found means of actively secreting oxygen inwards. It was a further instance of man's remarkable capacity for adapting himself to different surroundings. And the discovery, besides being of great value to science, is of high importance to the mountaineering world in general. Mountaineers need only allow themselves sufficient time for acclimatization and they may fearlessly attack any of the giants of the Himalaya or the Andes. They need no longer fear that the deficiency of oxygen in the air may be a conclusive obstacle to their attaining the highest altitudes.

A third expedition was organized in 1924, again under the leadership of General Bruce, with Colonel Norton as second in command. They reached nearer the summit than the previous expedition—Norton and Somervell attaining an altitude of slightly over 28,000 feet. But, as is well known, it ended in great tragedy. That magnificent mountaineer, Mallory, with his younger companion Irvine, lost their lives in a forlorn attempt to reach the summit carrying oxygen. They were last seen high up on the mountain "going strong for the top"; but they never returned, and nothing is known of how they lost their lives.

For a second time an Everest expedition had failed

to achieve its object. Norton and Somervell would undoubtedly have reached higher if they had not had to exhaust themselves before making their final effort by rescuing some marooned porters. But the expedition was not altogether fruitless. It had taught the climbers more about the mountain and about acclimatization at high altitudes. The experience of Odell, for example, in twice climbing to an altitude of 27,000 feet and spending ten days above 23,000 feet, was a valuable indication of human capacity of adaptation. And the porters also had been able to carry higher. They had enabled Norton and Somervell to start from a tent pitched at an altitude of 26,800 feet—higher than the summit of Nanga Parbat.

At the actual moment of turning back from further effort to reach the summit, Everest climbers have no sense of disappointment—only a feeling of relief. Through the shortage of oxygen their susceptibilities are dulled, and they have so exhausted themselves that they are almost dying men. For the time being they are indifferent to success or failure. But once they are back at even the 15,000-feet level of the plains of Tibet their keenness revives. And before Norton had returned to Darjiling he had cabled to the Everest Committee asking that an expedition might be organized to make another attempt. Application was therefore made to the Tibetan Government. But it was not favourably received. The gods of the mountains were evidently displeased, and they should not be again disturbed.

So for some years no more expeditions were possible. But quite unexpectedly, in August 1932, came the news that the Tibetan Government were again willing to allow an expedition to proceed to Everest. And as the Everest Committee had been kept in being all the time, and a sum of £5,000 preserved for equipping any new expedition, preparations could forthwith be undertaken.

The years had passed, and neither Norton nor Somervell or any member of the previous expeditions would be fit to reach the summit. But it was hoped that Norton would at least be able to lead the expedition. This, however, was not feasible, as he had only recently been appointed to an important military post. So the choice for leadership fell upon Hugh Ruttledge, who had for five years held civil charge of the Himalayan District of Almora. Besides being an expert Alpine climber, he had made ascents in the Himalaya, and knew Himalayan peoples. He was too old to be of those who would make the final assault. But he was an ideal man for organizing and leading an Everest expedition.

For the actual assault an ideal man was also available. Since the attacks on Everest had begun, interest in Himalayan mountaineering had greatly increased. Three German expeditions had been sent out to attempt Kangchenjunga, 28,150 feet. And Frank Smythe had accompanied one of these. He had also himself attacked and conquered the great peak, Kamet, 25,447 feet, and was still only thirty-three years old. He was therefore the very man to make the supreme effort. Others with less, though considerable, mountaineering experience, were got together, and, determining to make an earlier start than the former expeditions, Ruttledge managed to get away from Darjiling by March 5, 1933.

The vexed question of the use of oxygen had again been considered, and the expedition did take some light cylinders containing oxygen for use as a stimulant or restorative. But there was no intention to make a regular oxygen attempt as in the two previous expeditions, and Ruttledge made slow acclimatization the keynote of the expedition. Previous expeditions had proved that men did acclimatize themselves to high altitude conditions. But they also showed that the acclimatization to be effective must be gradual. Climbers must not rush the mountain. They must take their time about it. This was Ruttledge's idea. And he accordingly planned, by making an earlier start from Darjiling than previous expeditions had made, to reach the Base Camp earlier and thus allow of a more leisurely progress up the East Rongbuk Glacier to the foot of the mountain, so that the climbers might all the time be slowly acclimatizing themselves to high altitude conditions. Then it was hoped that when the time came for the final effort to be made they would be fitter for it than Norton and Somervell had been. They were to be, as Ruttledge put it, "at the top of their form."

This was his idea as far as "slow acclimatization" was concerned. But two other factors had to be reckoned with. One was deterioration. From excessive cold, from incessant biting winds, from sleeplessness, worry, high altitude irritability, headaches, unpalatable food, and general discomfort, deterioration sets in, and may counteract all the good that is being done by slow acclimatization. A man may arrive at the 27,000-feet level beautifully acclimatized but too weak and depressed to make any decent effort to reach the summit. The second opposing factor was the weather. Only a very short time is available for an attack on Everest. Before the beginning of May it is too appallingly cold. And after the beginning of June the monsoon sets in, smothers the mountain in snow, and renders climbing impossible. But at any day in that month the most terrible blizzard may arise and clamp the climbers down for two or three days. So, in order to seize a favourable spell of good weather, an attack might be necessary before the climbers were acclimatized to the very highest altitudes. Or, when they were acclimatized, they might be detained by a blizzard so long that they would have deteriorated in physical—and perhaps, also, in mental—condition.

These were the problems Ruttledge had to face, and he deliberately made out his plan of campaign before he entered Tibet. One would think that the best time to elaborate the plan would be on the march across Tibet, when the whole party was collected together and they could discuss it out between them. But experience has shown that during that march both leader and climbers are much too occupied to be able to give the necessary concentration of mind to a problem. Most careful calculations have to be made as to the formation and supply of camps on the glacier and the mountain, the relief of porters, and the rota of climbers: and these calculations are best made in the calmer atmosphere of England before the start is made.

On March 8, 1933, the expedition left Darjiling. On 16th April they arrived at Rongbuk Monastery, 16,000 feet, and on the 17th they reached Base Camp near the end of the Rongbuk Glacier, which flowed down from Everest. By 21st April, Camp I. on the glacier was in full occupation. At Camp II., 19,800 feet, fifty degrees of frost was experienced. And by 2nd May Camp III. was definitely established at an altitude of 21,000 feet at the head of the glacier, a mile from the ice slope which leads up to the North Col, 23,000 feet. It was not a rapid advance. But it had been part of Ruttledge's design that the progress up the glacier should be slow, so that each man might have four days in each camp in order to acclimatize, and also in order that Camp III. might be stocked so completely as to be practically independent of the Base Camp and able to victual the higher camps.

All, so far, had gone according to plan. But now the most difficult part of the whole ascent, viz. the climb on the North Col, lay before them, and they soon found that the slopes had very much changed—and changed for the worse—since the 1924 expedition. In place of the old route was a shining slope of ice. A most difficult and dangerous piece of mountaineering must be undertaken. Regular working parties had to be formed, and the slopes attacked day after day till a way up had been made. Each member in turn would, for about twenty minutes, take the lead and cut steps ; and while he was doing this the others would drive in stakes and fix ropes. For over 1,000 feet this work had to be done, and it took from 8th May to the 15th.

No sooner was this accomplished than a storm came on which stopped all work till the 20th. Thus were five most valuable days lost. At the same time came news that the monsoon was active in the Bay of Bengal—a good fortnight before it was due. What now should be done ? If the climbers made a rush to reach the top before the monsoon broke, they would probably find themselves insufficiently acclimatized, and be incapable of achieving their object. On the other hand, if they went leisurely up the mountain, acclimatizing as they went, they might find the monsoon bursting on them before they could make the final effort.

In this emergency Ruttledge himself went up to Camp IV. on the 21st—a good performance for a man of forty-eight—and decided that on the next day an effort should be made to establish Camp V. at not less than 25,500 feet, and on the following day establish Camp VI. On the morning of the 22nd Everest stood out clear, the face was free of snow, and there was little wind. The party were happy. The sun was shining brightly, and prospects were good. In these circumstances the climb went well. By one o'clock Camp V. had been pitched at 25,700 feet on an excellent platform. And if weather held it was the intention to establish Camp VI. the next day at about 27,400 feet.

But the weather did not hold. Another gale sprang up. Wyn Harris and Wager, who were to have gone on to establish Camp VI., stayed at Camp V. during 23rd May. In the meanwhile, encouraged by an apparent clearing in the sky, Smythe and Shipton had set out from Camp IV. They had thought that Wyn Harris and Wager had gone on, but on arrival, finding them still there and no room for the two pairs of climbers, a decision had to be made as to which pair should return to Camp IV. It was decided that Wyn Harris and Wager should return.

On 24th May the mountain was a terrible sight. A full gale was blowing. The face of the mountain was continually blotted from view in racing mist and snow.

A gruelling crisis was now on. While outside conditions were at their cruellest, and inwardly all tended to lethargy, firm decisions had to be taken—and decisions involving immediate action. For indecision would be as likely to lead to disaster as the silliest action. Smythe and Shipton at Camp V. could not be left there indefinitely, or they would starve. Nor could headquarters at Camp IV. stay there long. They might have to retreat. But if they retreated, how could they ever get down those terrible ice-slopes in a blizzard? Everest was mercilessly tightening the screw on these presumptuous intruders.

On the morning of the 25th she did, however, relax a little—just enough to make the climbers think there was still some hope. So, with Ruttledge himself leading and taking the brunt of the work in order to save the younger men for the yet harder work ahead, a party of five climbers and ten porters set out to re-victual Camp V. But by the time they had reached the North Col itself the wind had risen again, and, in the words of Ruttledge, "poured over in what seemed one solid stream of cold." It was torture. It pained the eyes in spite of protecting goggles. It imprisoned the limbs in a grip like that of fast-running icy water. Every upward step was a battle. And worst of all was the searing cold of the air drawn into over-driven lungs.

Some way up the ridge above the North Col the party met Smythe descending from Camp V. There had been some hope early that morning that he might be able to continue the upward effort and establish Camp VI., and the porters themselves had been willing to make the effort. Later, however, the wind began to rise again, the cold was intense, a storm was threatening, and Smythe and Shipton decided to retreat to the North Col and recuperate for another effort later on. As it was, every man of the eight picked porters was more or less suffering from frost-bite. The intention of re-stocking Camp V. was abandoned, and both parties now returned to Camp IV.

Arrived there, they might well have decided to give up the attempt on the mountain. All the nicely-calculated plans had miscarried. If Ruttledge had planned to be early on the mountain so had the monsoon. And Everest herself was at her fiercest. The porters had had terrible days at Camp V., and were suffering much pain. Camp IV.—situated just under the North Col — was becoming dangerous through little snow avalanches falling on the ledge on which it was situated. And the weather was still threatening. But retreat could not be thought of. The assaulting party might have to be reorganized. Fresh plans might have to be made. But the attack must continue.

Details of the new plans were worked out on 26th May. And to avoid the danger from avalanches a small camp was established on the Col itself. It was a frightfully exposed position ; but it was safe. And there the assaulting parties would remain while Ruttledge and others escorted the frost-bitten porters down to Camp III.

May 28th began well. Hope revived of an interval of fine weather before the monsoon set in ; and Wyn Harris, Wager, Birnie, and Longland, with twelve freshly-selected porters, set out from the North Col to re-establish Camp V. They reached the old position in five hours, and devoted the rest of the day to cooking, brewing hot drinks, and filling thermos flasks in readiness for the next day's breakfast.

On 29th May the early morning was very cold, with a biting wind whistling across the ridge. Would the porters be able and willing to carry loads still higher, and establish a Camp VI. well above the 27,000-feet level? This was the anxious question which the porters themselves alone could answer. On the last expedition it was only after four hours' persuasion that they could be induced to make this fearful effort. But since then the spirit of these wonderful hillmen had greatly changed. The thing had been done once, so why should it not be done again? Moreover, a strong esprit-de-corps had sprung up among them. Their predecessors had made a name for Sherpas and Bhutias. That name must be preserved and enhanced. Pride forbade them decline to make the effort. The eight "tigers" were ready and willing to go.

On account of the bitter cold and because the thermos flasks had not been able to keep the drinks hot during the night so that fresh drinks had to be brewed, a start was not made till 8 a.m. Then, leaving Birnie to act as support at Camp V., Wyn Harris, Wager, and Longland, with eight porters carrying ten pounds each, proceeded up the north ridge. At the end of every fifty minutes a ten minutes' halt was made, and, including this halt, the pace of ascent was 400 feet an hour. All went well, and the only difficulty was to find a spot sufficiently large and sufficiently level on which one Meade tent, seven feet long and four feet wide, could be pitched. The whole mountain-side was of steeply-sloping slabs; and the utmost that could be found was a fairly pronounced ledge, sloping outwards, clogged with snow, and nowhere more than three feet wide. A kind of platform was built up on this. The little ten-pound tent was anchored on it as securely as possible, four sleeping-bags, provisions for four days for four men, and some cooking-pots were deposited in it; and Camp VI., at an altitude of 27,400 feet, was established. A great mountaineering feat in itself.

This having been accomplished, Wyn Harris and Wager were left there, while Longland conducted the eight porters back to the North Col. Left to themselves they would, in their care-free way, have gaily dashed down the mountain by the nearest way and inevitably come to disaster. As it was, Longland, only by the display of the greatest mountain skill, brought them safely into camp. For suddenly—and literally "out of the blue"—a furious storm of wind and snow arose. At one moment all was peaceful. The next, Nature seemed to go mad. The wind rose to a scream. The snow tore past in blinding sheets. The men's goggles iced-up and had to be discarded. Then their eyelashes froze together. No landmarks could be seen through the racing snow. Some of the more exhausted porters sat down, unable longer to endure the fury of the wind. But they had to be urged on till at last a little tent was seen. It was Camp V., which they had left in the morning and in which Smythe and Shipton had now arrived. Two of the most exhausted porters were left here. Then Longland conducted the remainder down to the North Col, which he reached just before dark at the very limit of his own endurance.

The stage was thus once more set for an assault on

the summit. Wyn Harris and Wager were at Camp VI., 27,400 feet, ready to make an attempt next day. Smythe and Shipton were at Camp V., ready to follow on. Birnie was at Camp V., in support. And Longland, Crawford, and McLean were at the North Col. This was the position on 29th May. How it developed must be the story of another chapter.

North Col Camp
and the north-east shoulder of Mount Everest.

Chapter III

THE FINAL EFFORT

WYN HARRIS and Wager did not make a good start on the 30th. They had had a disturbed night. They had slept badly, and had woken up at 4.30 with a poor appetite and very thirsty, for on Everest the air is extremely dry, and water in quantity is not available, as the snow never melts. It was found, too, that the thermos flask had not been able to keep its contents warm, and they had to spend an hour in melting snow for water over a "cooker." This done, they had a light meal of Brand's essence of chicken, tinned loganberries, biscuit, and condensed milk. While they were consuming this very invalid-like repast their frozen boots were being thawed over another "cooker." And by 5.40 a.m., arrayed in their windproof over-garments, they were ready to emerge from their tent and tackle the climb to the summit.

The sun was not yet shining on their side of the mountain, and during the first hour they suffered much from the cold. Also, the excessive panting necessitated by the shortage of oxygen at this altitude of between 27,000 feet and 28,000 feet, caused a rapid loss of bodily heat, and they both felt symptoms of approaching frost-bite.

Their intention was to reach the crest of the ridge, and, as Mallory had purposed, proceed along it to the final pyramid and up that to the summit, 1,600 feet above their camp, and about a mile and a quarter distant. With a whole day before them this seemed a fairly reasonable proposition.

But the line along the crest was found to be impracticable. They came up against a dark grey precipice, smooth and holdless. It was impossible to proceed farther. Their only course was to climb along the side of the mountain, as Norton and Somervell had done some years before. Even this, though, was both difficult and dangerous. They had to pass over snow-covered sloping slabs much like the tiles on the roof of a house. And, as the slope ended in a sheer precipice, a slip would have landed them on a glacier ten thousand feet below.

Round a corner they reached a great snow couloir, or gully, which runs down from the final pyramid. Here they came upon a very awkward fifty feet of powdery snow which gave no support to the feet. It was almost the most dangerous part of the whole ascent. At terrible risk they were able to cross this obstacle and to creep slowly and carefully along for another 150 feet, when they reached the edge of a smaller gully, where the snow was particularly deep and soft. Wyn Harris attempted to cross it, but soon came to the conclusion that the limit of reasonable climbing had been reached.

It was now 12.30 p.m. They were at an altitude of approximately 28,100 feet, and therefore still about a thousand feet below the summit. At the very least four hours would be required to reach it, and such a period would not leave them time to return. Their only course, then, was to give up the attempt and return to Camp VI. They reached it at 4 p.m., and found Smythe and Shipton there. So, after telling them the results of their enterprise, they proceeded to Camp V., where they spent the night.

The first attempt had failed. It had been brought to a standstill at approximately the same point that Norton had reached. It now remained for Smythe and Shipton to make a final effort. They had had a rough time on the way up to Camp VI. on the previous two days. The cold had been intense, stinging clouds of snow had reduced visibility to a few yards, and they had been glad enough to escape from the blizzard into the shelter of Camp V. During the afternoon the blizzard had increased in fury, and the swirling snow was seen tearing across the face of Everest. Fortunately, the blizzard had blown itself out in the night, the day had dawned fine, and they had been able to reach Camp VI. without serious difficulty a few hours before Wyn Harris and Wager's return there after their attempt on the summit.

The evening was peaceful. But the two climbers passed a restless, uncomfortable night, and awoke tired and with the depression which comes from want of sufficient oxygen. As daylight came on the wind rose and snow began to fall. It was impossible to attempt the summit. By the afternoon a blizzard was raging, and they could only stay in the tent. The next day dawned clear but so cold they could not get into their frozen boots and windproof clothing before 6.30 a.m. What their total clothing was has been described by Smythe. He wore one Shetland vest, a thick flannel shirt, a thick camel-hair sweater, six light Shetland pullovers, two long pairs of Shetland pants, flannel trousers, and, over all, a silk-lined "Grenfell" windproof suit. His head was protected by a light Shetland balaclava helmet, and an outer helmet of Grenfell cloth. And he wore four pairs of Shetland socks and stockings. The climbing boots were broad and lightly nailed, yet capable of gripping tightly on the sloping slabs. And on his hands he wore woollen fingerless gloves, and over them a pair of South African lambskin gloves.

This pair of climbers did not, like the previous pair, attempt to go along the crest. They kept below it, ascending slightly till they reached a gently-sloping terrace of scree, on which they noted a camp might be pitched. Passing beneath what is known as "the first step" in the crest, they continued along a gradually narrowing series of ledges. And here Shipton, who even before starting had complained of stomach trouble, now suddenly succumbed. So Smythe, like Norton years before, had to go on alone towards the summit.

Presently he came to the great couloir. In general angle it was exceedingly steep, and two or three hundred feet lower down ended in a sheer precipice. To his surprise the couloir at the point where he entered was filled with hard snow, in which he had to cut a dozen steps, pausing frequently for breath. Having successfully crossed the great couloir at 10 a.m., he made his way towards the subsidiary couloir, which makes the only breach in the otherwise impregnable black band of rock that runs across the northern face of Everest. Smythe intended to make a steep ascending traverse into the subsidiary couloir, enter it as high as possible, and thence follow it through the breach on to the face of the final pyramid.

This was his intention. But the climbing, which up to then had been more dangerous than difficult, now became both difficult and dangerous. The newly-fallen snow had accumulated on every part that was not too steep to hold it. It was soft like flour, loose like castor sugar, and of such consistency that it could not hold the foot and so prevent a slip. In places he sank into it knee-deep, frequently even thigh-deep. Sometimes he had to grope about in the snow for holds. At other times he would shovel the snow away altogether until roughnesses in the slabs beneath were exposed. It was work, even Smythe says, of the most arduous and exacting nature.

By 11 a.m. he had gained only fifty feet in height, and reached about the same place as Wyn Harris and Wager had reached two days previously, and as Norton had reached in 1924. The attainment of the summit was clearly out of the question, and all he could do was to return to his old camp. Even this was a tedious business. But by 1.30 p.m. he reached it, and while Shipton, who had by now recovered, went on down the mountain, Smythe decided to remain on it for the night.

An hour later a sudden and terrific storm broke. A whirling smother of snow raged across the slabs. But towards sundown the wind dropped again, and Smythe settled down to spend a night alone at 27,400 feet above sea-level. He turned in at 6 p.m., and it was not until 7 a.m. the next morning that he awoke—a most excellent refutation of the old argument that men would not be able to sleep at an altitude above 20,000 feet.

The morning was the coldest he ever remembered. But the weather was calm, and there was little movement in the sea of monsoon clouds beneath him. When he started down the mountain there appeared to be nothing unusual in the air. Then, all of a sudden, a gust of such strength struck him that he was nearly carried off his feet. There followed another, and another gust, and soon a terrific storm was raging. "It was impossible to face the storm for more than a moment or two, for goggles soon iced-up, and the driving snow stung like whip-lashes." The wind increased to such a strength as Smythe had never before experienced on any mountain. The air was filled with driving snow. It was seldom possible to see more than a yard or two. Often he was reduced to crawling on hands and knees ; and several times he was swept from his balance and only saved by his axe from a fatal slide.

The cold, too, was terrible. In spite of all he was wearing it seemed to clasp the whole of him in its grip. He felt a deadly numbness creeping up his body. And it might have gone ill with him if he had not been able to get to the shelter behind the crest of the north ridge. There the horrid deadening feeling slowly left his body, and circulation painfully returned to his hands. Then he was able to continue the descent, and eventually reached Camp IV.

The bolt had been shot. Man had had his go : and had failed. He had gone all out, but on three occasions he had been brought up at the same point, and that point a thousand feet below the summit. He had not reached the base of the final pyramid. He may have had bad luck. He may have encountered exceptionally severe seasons. Certainly, in his last attempt the monsoon had broken weeks before the usual time. The cold had been appalling. The wind terrific. The snow enough to make progress on the sloping slabs in the highest degree dangerous. Still, there is the fact that from one cause or another man had not been able to reach the summit.

Should he therefore be content? He has shown that, anyhow, he can get to 28,000 feet with what one might almost say comparative ease. Should he leave it at that? Some think he should. Some mountaineers think so. Writing of Mallory's attempt and its still unknown issue, Mr. Irving says that we may never know whether the cross of victory should be placed by materialists at 28,000 or 29,000 feet. He asks: "Does it really matter? . . . Do we destroy nothing by using all this mass of men and material to conquer Everest?" And he quotes Mallory himself as writing after the second expedition: "How can I help rejoicing in the yet undimmed splendour, the undiminished glory, the unconquered supremacy of Everest!"

But do these words ring true? Is there not a "literary" twang about them? Would mountaineers really grieve if the spirit of man proved itself capable of facing the material obstacles presented by the mountain? Thousands of men, and even hundreds of women, must by now have stood on the summit of Mont Blanc. But can any one truly affirm that its glory is less now than it was before De Saussure climbed it? And if the next Everest expedition proves successful, would Everest be in any way less impressive than it is at present?

The actual climber of Everest, at the actual moment when he is standing on the summit, will have no appreciation of its glory, or even pride in himself. From want of oxygen he will be in no state to feel anything. It will take all his remaining energies to enable him mechanically to descend the mountain. But once he is down at sea-level again, how will he be able to do anything else than rejoice that he has been able to carry to final fruition what his predecessors had prepared for him, and that as the representative of man he has been able to put the mountain under his foot ?

None more than he will respect and admire the mountain. Its glory and splendour will even for him be in no way dimmed. And for the rest of us, while our pride in the spirit of man will have risen, will not the mountain still stand out in untarnishable glory ?

Did not Ruttledge, therefore, strike the authentic note of the mountaineer when he wrote : "I assume without hesitation that the attempt to climb Mount Everest will be continued. We cannot leave the work unfinished."

At any rate, this is the view taken by the unrepentant Everest Committee. And, again under the leadership of Ruttledge, a still more determined effort is to be made in 1936 to reach the summit. But before we estimate the prospects of its success we should examine the results which have already been attained.

CHAPTER IV

RESULTS

TIME after time the climbers have failed to reach the summit of Everest. Immense preparations have been made in England. Intense thought has been given to the project. Hundreds of local men have been engaged in transporting the climbers to the mountain. And the climbers themselves have been ready to endure the severest physical strain and run every risk—even the risk of losing their lives. Yet the mountain remains unconquered.

But if the expeditions have failed in achieving their supreme object they have not been wholly fruitless of results. The climbers have not reached 29,000 feet ; but three times they have reached 28,000 feet. And this is an advance of more than 3,000 feet upon anything which had been achieved before. It gives promise that it is only a matter of time before the last thousand feet will be climbed.

And in the process of climbing to 28,000 feet the climbers have unwittingly given evidence of one scientific fact of great importance—the fact that the human organism can adapt itself to the atmospheric conditions prevailing at the highest terrestrial altitudes. Life is one long process of adaptation of the living being to its surroundings. But that adaptation can only be effected within certain limits. The human organism can adapt itself to a great variety of surrounding conditions. But it cannot adapt itself indefinitely. If the temperature is too low or too high the organism succumbs. So also is it with altitude. If a man were suddenly transported to an altitude of 50,000 feet, or even 29,000 feet, above sea-level he would die. On the other hand, practical experience has shown that if he is not transported suddenly to a great height, but ascends slowly, he can gradually adapt himself to the conditions of high altitude. The only question has been, how high would be the altitude to which men could thus adapt themselves? When De Saussure ascended Mont Blanc, which is less than 16,000 feet in height, he and his companions puffed and blew and made very heavy going of the altitude. Nowadays nothing is thought of it. And when the Everest expeditions were started, though it was known that man could ascend to anyhow the 25,000-feet level, for the Duke of Abruzzi had reached 24,600 feet, it was still very doubtful whether he could, without the aid of oxygen, ascend to even 26,000 feet; and scientific men predicted that he probably would be unable to sleep at 23,000 feet—and if he could not sleep at that altitude there seemed to be little prospect of his being able to reach the summit. But the expeditions have proved that man can adapt himself to the conditions at even the 28,000-feet level. Further, they have shown that men can carry light loads as high as 27,400 feet. And Smythe slept soundly for thirteen hours at that height.

This fact that man can adapt himself to the highest terrestrial altitude conditions is one very valuable result of the Everest expeditions. We know something about ourselves—something to our advantage—which we did not know before.

And what a change in men's views this is may be judged when we look back on Mallory saying after the first expedition that he supposed that the limit of acclimatization must be somewhere about 21,000 feet; and on Somervell (a medical man as well as a climber) saying, when the expedition of 1922 started, that he was personally of opinion that nobody could exist without oxygen at a height above 25,000 or 26,000 feet.

Now it has been discovered that if the higher altitudes are not rushed, but approached gradually, the human body, with its proverbial capacity for adapting itself to varying conditions, will adapt itself to increasing deficiency of oxygen in the air. The airman who flies over Everest has no need to adapt himself, for enough oxygen to make up the deficiency is carried with him in the aeroplane, and all he has to do is to suck it in during the few hours which it takes to fly over Everest from the plains of India and return there. But the climber, if he were to trust to such artificial supply of oxygen, would have to carry it on his back in a most cumbersome apparatus. And the value of the discovery that man can adapt himself to the deficiency of oxygen lies in the fact that he can climb to the highest altitudes without carrying this apparatus. He can do without it and yet reach the 28,000-feet level.

He can only do this, however, if he approaches the higher altitudes by slow degrees. He must not rush the mountain. He must give his body time, slowly and gradually, to adapt itself to the new conditions. The previous expeditions had gone at it too fast, and they suffered in consequence. They had headaches, they got blue in the face, they became irritable, they lost their appetites, they panted, they felt lassitude, they could not concentrate their minds, they became generally miserable. Even Somervell spoke of peevishness at 22,000 feet, and at 27,000 feet he cared very little whether he got to the top or not. Ruttledge, profiting by his experience, gave his expedition more time. He conducted the march across Tibet, and the establishment of camps on the East Rongbuk Glacier and the North Col, 23,000 feet, at such moderate speed as would allow the maximum possible number of climbers to reach an attacking position unstrained and at the very top of their form. He believed that if only they would take their time in going up the East Rongbuk Glacier they would arrive on the North Col with plenty of reserve in hand. So no impatience, or spell of fine weather, was allowed to turn them from the predetermined plan of spending at least four days at every camp on the way up the East Rongbuk Glacier in order that their bodies might accustom themselves to the progressive decrease of oxygen in the air they breathed.

Their efforts, Raymond Green, the medical officer of the expedition, considered, were rewarded to a remarkable degree. There was absence of serious respiratory distress. Except in the case of one slow acclimatizer, disordered breathing passed off rapidly. Of the fourteen climbers, thirteen reached the North Col without having experienced serious discomfort. Above the North Col proper acclimatization was made impossible by the weather and by the nature of the ground. Yet even the distress in breathing felt by the climbers was not great. And what is very remarkable, considering what we were told of the climbers on previous expeditions requiring seven or eight or nine breaths between each step at the higher altitudes, climbers on the 1933 expedition needed only two or three breaths to a step—even above 27,000 feet—and found frequent halts unnecessary. Their appetites were excellent, and at the highest camps they were clamouring for substantial food in face of the delicate fare provided. Headaches were uncommon. They slept well. As we have seen, Smythe, after his climb to 28,100 feet, slept for thirteen hours in the tent at 27,400 feet. Lassitude was less. They were occasionally irritable, one is glad to hear, in case they might be thought too angelic. But only those who went above 27,000 feet experienced any mental deterioration. And, in general, they are reported as being " remarkably fit, cheerful, and energetic, even at camps above the North Col."

With the porters the same improvement was noted.

They were ready to go to the highest camps. There was no difficulty in making them start in the morning, even under the worst conditions. And there were no cases of mountain sickness.

How is it that this acclimatization or accustoming of the human body to the progressive decrease of the oxygen in the air it inhales takes place? The most important way is by an increased ventilation of the lungs. There has to be deeper breathing. The first deep breathing of the ascending climber is probably caused by the direct effects of oxygen-lack. But this renders the respiratory centre in the brain more susceptible to changes in the acidity of the blood. And at the same time it washes carbon dioxide out of the blood and so lowers its acidity. This has to be rectified. And the kidneys have to rectify it by secreting more alkali and so making the blood more acid again. The kidneys only learn this function slowly. But when they do acclimatization has taken place. This process of acclimatization is assisted by an increase in the number of red corpuscles, whose function it is to carry oxygen. And possibly there may be active secretion of oxygen by the lung epithelium. By these chemical changes in the body does it adapt itself gradually, and within certain limits, to the changing conditions.

And the condition of the climbers in 1933 at 28,000 feet was so good that in Raymond Green's opinion there is little doubt of their capacity, in good condition, to climb Everest without oxygen.

Nevertheless, the benefits of acclimatization do not

meet all the necessities of the situation. Even the most acclimatized Everest climber is not as fit as a climber on Mont Blanc. From the snow, the cold, the contending with blizzards, the labour of cutting steps in ice, the having for any reason to push on at a faster rate, the discomfort of tiny tents, the want of fresh food, the monotonous and badly-cooked food, and even from acclimatization itself—from all these causes deterioration sets in and the time comes when the climbers lose their appetite and weight, and become less energetic. In all probability prolonged shortage of oxygen is directly or indirectly the most important cause of this deterioration, says Raymond Green, and acclimatization, itself originally due to oxygen-lack, may carry deterioration with it as a noxious by-product.

The good effects of acclimatization are, therefore, to some extent counterbalanced by the bad effects of deterioration, and if climbers stayed for too long at the higher altitudes deterioration might outweigh the good of acclimatization. But for the short periods it is alone possible to remain on the upper part of Everest, the advantages of acclimatization are very apparent.

It is not only the bodies of individual climbers that have become acclimatized to the supreme altitudes: their minds also are becoming acclimatized. When nothing was known for certain about accessibility of the summit, when no one knew whether a man, with or without the aid of oxygen, could climb at such altitudes as 28,000 and 29,000 feet, when we knew nothing about the state of the mountain itself, the climbers' minds were full of uncertainty. Now, as the result of our expeditions, men know the mountain, and their minds are thoroughly acclimatized to the 28,000-feet level. On two expeditions men have reached it. There is no uncertainty about it. It is now regarded as the starting-point for the real climb. And this acclimatization of the mind, as well as of the body, will be of great value to the climbers on their next attempt to reach the summit.

It will also be of value to all others who attempt to reach the summits of other peaks. The fact that men have actually climbed to the altitude of the highest peaks next after Everest—to the altitude of Kangchenjunga and K_2—will help to acclimatize the minds of climbers of all lesser heights. In regard to the effect of altitude their minds will be at rest.

The experience gained on Mont Blanc is being repeated on Mount Everest. Men still feel certain altitude effects in climbing Mont Blanc, but they accept the discomforts as all in the day's work, and do not take them so seriously as De Saussure on his first climb did. It is the same with the Everest climbers. The last expedition, fortified with the knowledge that Norton and Somervell had reached 28,000 feet, went at the mountain with a far greater assurance than their predecessors. They suffered, but they did not bother unduly about the suffering. And this greater composure of mind reacted on the body. They went more easily about their task.

The spirit of mankind, as a whole, has also been affected for the good by these undaunted efforts to reach the earth's highest summit. It is not only a few Everest climbers that have been heartened by it. In the words of the Bavarian climber, Bauer, the whole world was thrilled by the spectacle of men gallantly facing every danger in their struggle to attain the summit. And the spectacle had the effect on Bauer himself of inspiring him to lead an expedition to attack Kangchenjunga, the third highest of the Himalayan giants. These Everest expeditions gave, in fact, what their organizers anticipated they would give, a tremendous impetus to Himalayan climbing. They have attracted the attention of the climbing world to the Himalaya. Every year now some great expedition comes out from Europe, and all are inspired to emulate the pertinacity of the Everest climbers.

Mountaineering is undertaken on a vaster scale, and has a more extended range. Climbing in the Lake District in England can be both as difficult and dangerous as climbing in the Alps or on Everest. But mountaineering in the Alps is on a definitely grander scale than mountaineering in England. Similarly, while there may be just as much difficulty and danger in certain climbs in the Alps as on Everest, yet mountaineering in the Himalaya is on a wholly vaster scale than mountaineering in Switzerland. Not only is it that the peaks are, roughly speaking, twice the height, but their whole mass is many times greater. Everything in the Himalaya is on a grander scale. Long marches have to be made to reach even the base of a Himalayan giant. And from the base no climber can reach the summit and be back in a single day: he has to spend many days and nights upon the face of the mountain. Avalanches are on a more colossal scale. Both cold and heat are intenser: the blizzards more terrific. And all this means that the mountaineer is tested more severely. The very utmost is elicited from him. For the time being he may be so exhausted physically as to be unable to experience the joys of mountaineering. Before his eyes may be one of the grandest scenes in the world, but life within him may be at so low an ebb that he may be capable only of a hasty, weary glance at the surrounding mountains. Yet the time will come when he will be grateful for having been forced to be his physically utmost. The impress which the mountains will have made upon his soul will begin to take effect. And then he will become aware of what mountaineering on the Himalayan scale means in joy as well as suffering.

The Everest expeditions have had a stimulating effect upon Europeans. They have also stirred the peoples of the Himalaya themselves. From the fact that the men who live all their lives in sight of the Himalayan peaks have never had the enterprise to climb even the lesser giants it might be assumed that they have little of the spirit of adventure in them. And certainly they cannot possess it in very high degree. Yet there is plenty of it there once it is aroused. A leader has only to come forward and they will eagerly flock to him. And not only for the pay but for the name and fame, and for the joy of great adventure. Such men are to be found right along the Himalaya. And the Everest expeditions have called out this latent and unsuspected spirit in them. The Himalayan people themselves are now thrilled with the idea of climbing the highest of all mountains. The lead has been given, and they are ready enough to follow it.

And between these Himalayan peoples and the European climbers a very noticeable spirit of comradeship has sprung up. And this may be taken as one of the most satisfactory of all the results of the expeditions. It might have been far otherwise. If these Himalayans had been treated as merely hired porters expected to give service in return for wages, but beyond that of no interest ; or if they had been bullied into action, Himalayan expeditions would have got a bad name among the Himalayan peoples, and each successive expedition would have found it harder to obtain porters. But it is to the everlasting credit of the Everest expeditions that they treated their porters as fellow human beings—and, what is more, as fellow mountaineers ; and the porters were quick to respond. The creation of this spirit of comradeship between European climbers and Himalayan peoples is a priceless achievement, with effects which will grow and multiply for good in the years to come.

If this result is due to any one man it is due to General Bruce. It is his great contribution to mountaineering. And it has been a life-work with him. He possesses a perfect genius for handling Himalayan peoples. His heart has always remained the heart of a boy. He bubbles over with boyish spirits even now. And this is exactly the temperament to suit the simple people of the Himalaya. All his service was passed in a Gurkha regiment stationed in the Himalaya ; and so devoted was he to his men that he would bring one or two of them home to England on leave. He would learn their folk-lore and legends too, and enter deeply into their attitude to life. So these men are at home and at ease with him. They know he knows them. They know he is aware of their naughtinesses. But they know also that he cares for them, that he will look after them and stand up for them and champion them. He may come down on them like a ton of bricks for any slackness or any misdeed ; but he will blaze out in righteous indignation at any ill-treatment of them or any reflection on them. And he will see to it that they are generously paid, amply equipped, and richly rewarded for good service done.

Bruce was too old to be climbing on Everest itself. There it was Norton who set the standard and established the code. He had nothing like the knowledge of Himalayan people that Bruce had, but he knew men in general, and had the gift of handling them. Especially had he engrained in him the principle that a leader must look after the least of every one of his followers before himself. He might be strict with them, he might vigorously suppress any laxity, but he would care for their welfare and stand by them in danger. And he did indeed stand by them on that notable occasion when four of them were marooned on the ice-fall of the North Col, and he, Somervell, and Mallory, at the risk of their lives, and at the risk of the success of the whole expedition, climbed up perilous ice-slopes to their rescue. By these and other deeds Norton and the other climbers established the tradition that these Himalayan porters were something more than carriers : they were fellow-mountaineers, comrades in high enterprise. And the porters on their side responded whole-heartedly to the treatment. They stood by the climbers as devotedly as the climbers stood by them. Thus was a comradeship of the mountain established.

These traditions the recent great German expeditions to the Himalaya have accepted and made their own. The leaders and members of those expeditions had already a strong sense of comradeship among themselves, for they had been accustomed to climbing together in their own mountains and in Switzerland. And, quickly recognizing the sterling qualities of the Himalayan porters, they soon came to embrace them, too, in their comradeship. There was, indeed, one lapse from the strict observance of such comradeship. In a great emergency two climbers left the porters to find their own way down a dangerous mountain-side. But the fact that the lapse was commented on in severest terms in German Alpine clubs is a clear enough indication of the high standard of dealing with Himalayan porters that German climbers have set themselves.

Between German and British climbers, also, a mountain comradeship has sprung up in the Himalaya. What rivalry there may be in ascending the highest summits is more in the nature of spirited emulation than of jealousy or hostility. Stern experience of the Himalaya has taught each what attainment means in the way of careful forethought, skill in mountain-craft, cheerful endurance of hardship, and readiness to risk and sacrifice. So each can admire and respect the deeds of the others, and all are joined together in the joy of great mountaineering.

In fostering this comradeship the Himalayan Club has played a prominent part. It cannot be said that the foundation of this Club was directly due to the Everest expeditions, yet it is certainly true that these expeditions did give an impetus to the idea of forming some kind of Himalayan association ; and members of Everest expeditions have done much to instil into the Club the true spirit of great mountaineering. And men like Kenneth Mason, who may not be skilled in the technique of mountain-craft as developed to such a high pitch of efficiency among Alpine climbers to-day, but who yet have wide and long experience of the Himalaya and a great love of the mountains and mountain people, were able to give to the Club a width of outlook which the mere climbing expert might not possess. And so it has come about that the Himalayan Club has been able to do much to aid the German Himalayan expeditions. It has welcomed them to India, entertained them, made advance arrangements, and collected porters for them, and in many different ways bound German and British and Himalayan mountaineers together in a common fellowship.

And what joins them together in this comradeship is not joy in conquest in any sense of that word which implies subjugation and keeping under foot. There is no question of trampling Everest to the ground. Everest will stand erect just as proudly as ever, after as before man's foot is placed on her summit, and will still possess the same power of demanding the utmost from men, and irresistibly charming them to her. What joins men together is the joy in conquest in the sense of mind acquiring an increasing supremacy over matter. The climber who first "conquers" Everest will probably be humbler than any other of those who have seen her, for he better than any one else will know what effort and sacrifice conquest of the mountain means. Yet he and all men will have quite legitimate pride in the triumph. It will be one more proof that man's capacities are growing, and that he need not be unduly awed by mere physical bulk. And it is this delight in a sense of expanding capacity which all can share that links mountaineers together.

Acclimatization of both mind and body to the highest altitudes and the creation of a spirit of comradeship among mountaineers in the Himalaya, and between them and the Himalayans, are some most valuable results of these elaborate expeditions. And with these results and the increased familiarity with the mountain in mind, we can estimate the chances of success of future expeditions.

Chapter V

1936 AND FUTURE PROSPECTS

NO further knowledge of the mountain itself was gained by the 1936 expedition. The monsoon set in "abnormally early," and they had no chance of climbing higher than the North Col. But in considering the prospects of success of any future expedition some short account of this year's frustrated attempt will at least show how dependent on the weather every expedition is.

Again under the leadership of Hugh Ruttledge, and with ample time for preparation, the 1936 expedition set out full of confidence. It included the well-tried and superb mountaineers Frank Smythe and Eric Shipton, the pair marked out for the first attempt on the summit. Another who had gone to 28,000 feet on Everest was Wyn Harris, while C. Kempson, a Marlborough master, Dr. C. B. Warren, and Lieutenant P. R. Oliver were also expected to go high.

Ruttledge's plan, worked out in detail before he left Darjiling, was to get to the Base Camp by the end of April, establish Camp IV. on the North Col on 22nd May, and make the first assault on, approximately, 25th May. Smythe and Shipton were to make this first assault, Wyn Harris and Kempson were to follow up and make the second assault if the first failed. Both pairs were to have oxygen for use at discretion. And, if neither of these parties succeeded, Warren and Oliver would make a fully organized attempt with oxygen.

It was recognized that the last two thousand feet presented great natural climbing difficulties. The great couloir is a gully of ice-covered rock, with steep slippery sides ; and, as we have already seen, no member of any of the previous expeditions had succeeded in crossing it. But Ruttledge hoped to improve upon previous expeditions by placing a camp a third of a mile nearer the summit. He hoped to place Camp VII. at about 27,800 feet. And he anticipated the pair of climbers would take about one hour to reach the great couloir, four hours to cross the couloir and climb the great buttress forming its west side, four hours to reach the summit from the top of the great buttress, and six hours to get back to Camp VII. If they set out at 6 a.m. they would be back at 7 p.m. ; and a lamp would be fixed on Camp VII. to guide them back.

This was the plan, based on the accumulated experience of the previous expeditions, which Ruttledge laid down. And all went well at the start, so that it looked as if, at last, success were in sight. They were able to get away from Gantok in Sikkim on 19th March and to go up the Sikkim valley to Kampa Jong instead of going round by Phari as the previous expeditions had done. On 27th April, after an easy march in splendid weather, they reached the old Base Camp ;

and an advance party occupied Camp I. on the East Rongbuk Glacier and began turning into the new Base Camp. The weather was exceptionally mild. The party was very fit and well acclimatized. By 6th May Camp II. was fully established. By 12th May Camp III. was stocked with everything required for operations on the mountain. On 13th May the route up the great ice-face of the North Col had been completed. On 15th May Smythe and Shipton occupied Camp IV. on the North Col. It had originally been intended that this Camp IV. should be established on 22nd May, and that the first assault should be made on 25th May. But things had gone so well that it was expected that the first assault on the mountain itself might be made about 17th May.

But here came the tragedy. Things had been too rosy. So far the weather had been marvellously quiet. From this time onward snow began to fall. On 15th May Smythe and Shipton with all porters had to return to Camp III. And owing to the continued snow, which rendered the upper slabs of rocks unclimbable for the time, the whole expedition had to be brought back to Camp I. on 21st May. On 24th May the monsoon, much before its normal time, had reached the mountain. It had not been kept back by the northerly winds which usually blow from Tibet, and had reached Everest in only four days from the Bay of Bengal. A slight lull in the monsoon, a strengthening of the winds from Tibet, and the sight of the snow being blown off the mountain in great sheets, revived the hopes of the expedition, and on 1st June they again advanced up the glacier. But conditions changed for the worse once more, and the party were not able to reach even the North Col.

Just one possibility remained. Perhaps a way on to the face of Everest might be found, not up the East Rongbuk Glacier, which all expeditions so far had used, but up the main Rongbuk Glacier. This line, therefore, was tried. And on 10th June the whole party encamped at the head of the main glacier and immediately under the north face of Everest, up which lay the only way to the summit. And if only that face could be reached the summit itself might be gained. For now the northerly winds were blowing in great strength. The newly fallen snow was being swept from the mountain. And Smythe and Wyn Harris did discover a way by which under certain conditions the North Col might be reached from this main Rongbuk Glacier direction. But again the snow fell, and lay so deep that it was evident that Everest could not be climbed this year.

Man was ignominiously beaten this time. He was not even permitted to set his foot on the mountain itself. Will he, therefore, give up the struggle? Will he admit that mountain can conquer man? Most assuredly not. Time after time he will renew the struggle. He will develop new technique. New ways of withstanding the cold and the wind. New ways of tackling the snow. Perhaps even a way of climbing by night. Some way or other will surely be found of overcoming those difficulties which these five initiatory

British expeditions have at least succeeded in bringing to light. And whether other expeditions be British, or German, or Italian, or of any other nationality; and whether they be organized by "Everest Committees," or be composed of individuals banded together for the time, like the Bauer and Merkl expeditions, the assault by man on the mountain will surely continue.

What actually remains is to climb the last thousand feet. When man is again able to reach so near the summit what difficulties will he still have to surmount?

Norton * says that the approach to the final pyramid from the highest camp does entail some danger. In preference to the way along the actual crest of the ridge running up to the summit he would prefer the route which he and Somervell followed, roughly parallel to the crest, but from 500 to 1,000 feet below it on the north face. It becomes steep and rather dangerous, though nowhere difficult, in and just west of the big couloir or gully which cuts off the final pyramid from the great north-east shoulder of the mountain. For about 200 feet the going on this route is very steep. The climber has delicately to find his way on overlying slabs approximating to the general slope of the mountain. And one gathers from the climbers' description that the general slope of the mountain approximates to the slope of the roof of a house. On these steeply-

* *Alpine Journal*, Vol. XXXVII.

sloping slabs there is often—perhaps generally—a sprinkling of snow; and herein lies the danger. For this sprinkling of snow conceals the footholds; and the snow itself, sheltered as it is from wind and sun, is powdery and of the consistency of coarse salt, and nowhere supports the foot.

Above the point which Norton reached along this route he says there is about 200 feet of steep, slabby rock, and then the climber would emerge on to the face of the final pyramid. The climbing on this 200 feet would be steeper than anything on rock below, and over portions of it there might be necessity for the climbers to move one at a time on a belayed rope. And this fact should not be forgotten in estimating times for both the ascent and descent. But after emerging on to the face of the final pyramid there should, in Norton's view, be no further difficulty up to the summit. And he considers that an average rate of from 200 to 250 feet an hour could be maintained by a fit party in climbing the last 1,000 feet of Everest.

Now, as we have seen, those who in 1933 followed Norton got no farther than he did in 1924. Wyn Harris and Wager, in the first attempt, and Smythe in the second attempt, were all three brought up at pretty well the same point that Norton reached. We have, therefore, no more direct knowledge of what difficulties the final pyramid may present. But we have a very carefully considered opinion by Smythe * on the final problem.

* *Alpine Journal*, Vol. XLVI. p. 42.

Smythe endorses Norton's view that the final pyramid should be approached by Norton's route and not by the crest. What he thinks would prove the crux of the climb would be the ascent of about 400 feet of the subsidiary couloir on to the face of the final pyramid, though possibly, as the snow in the couloir would almost certainly be soft and powdery, it might be necessary to utilize the rocks by the side of it. Owing to the direct nature of this climb up the couloir, rope could be used to advantage, and he would advise using rope on this portion of the climb, for not only is the route technically difficult, but it is one where a tired man on the descent from the summit might all too probably slip. Therefore he would advise that the climbers should carry with them, apart from what rope they may require for climbing purposes, at least 400 feet of the lightest line consistent with the necessary strength, and also some pitons. The climbers would wear leather belts, and on the descent thread the line through them.

Over the face of the final pyramid, at about 28,300 feet, the going may be found steep and fatiguing by reason of the broken nature of the mountain-side, says Smythe. But he anticipates that there would be no difficulty until the abrupt little wall leading up to the summit ridge is reached. This ridge must be some 200 yards in length, and if it is ascended at its eastern extremity there is a possibility that cornices may be encountered. So though the ridge, judged by Alpine standards, appears to be easy, Smythe recommends taking a piton and a length of spare line even to the summit in order to avoid risks on the descent.

Wyn Harris suggests, further, the advisability of carrying a very light oxygen apparatus from the highest camp to the foot of the subsidiary couloir. On the way to the couloir the oxygen would not be used. But for that crucial part of the whole way to the summit—that steep 400 feet leading up to the face of the final pyramid—the oxygen would be inhaled to give the climbers the necessary physical and mental stimulus. The oxygen apparatus would then be left at the top of the couloir, and the climbers would proceed on their own steam for the remaining 600 feet to the summit, while any oxygen that might be left would be used as a stimulus during the descent of that dangerous 400 feet.

Thus aided—or perhaps without the aid—Smythe assumes that an uphill speed of slightly over 200 feet an hour might be attained from the foot of the subsidiary couloir to the summit. If this could be done the summit would be reached at midday. The maximum safe limit for it to be reached would be about 2 p.m., for, taking into account the fatigue of the returning climbers, and the technical difficulties they would have to overcome, it is not probable that they would be able to descend at any faster rate than 300 feet an hour.

All this would be easy enough anywhere near the sea-level. But as onlookers of the struggle, we are brought up by the fact that, comparatively simple as the task might be to trained mountaineers like the

Everest climbers have all been, they have never been able even to begin the ascent of that last 1,000 feet. They have always been too exhausted by the time they reached the crucial point. Norton and Somervell were already done up through having to rescue the men marooned on the North Col. They were quite unfit for the supreme effort. Wyn Harris and Wager were also exhausted through having had first to explore the way to the crest route. And of the succeeding couple, Shipton was taken ill and could not accompany Smythe, and Smythe himself was anything but at the top of his form through having had to exert himself severely in making the way up the North Col.

So we must look a little farther back in our problem. We must see how we can get our climbers up to the crucial point 1,000 feet below the summit in fit form to tackle that really very dangerous and difficult 400 feet up the couloir, and the further 600 feet to the summit.

This leads us back to that counsel of perfection at which every Everest expedition religiously sets out—the need of keeping a pair in clover for the final effort. That has always been the theory. Obviously, those who will be expected to make the supreme effort should not be worn out in subsidiary work. In practice it has been found that Everest makes such tremendous demands upon the entire membership of the expeditions that it has not been possible to save up any particular climber. The ascent of that ice-fall from the North Col each year presents some new difficulty, necessitating the aid of the most skilful members if it is to be overcome. Porters have to be helped over some dangerous part, or rescued from some predicament into which they have fallen. One or more of the climbers fall ill or prove to be slow acclimatizers. Terrific blizzards suddenly spring up. From one or all of these causes the nicely-calculated plans for saving a pair for the final effort are sent flying off the mountain, and the crowning effort has had to be made with men so played-out as to be utterly incapable of reaching the summit and returning from it.

Still the effort to keep a pair fit must be continued—and continued with increased determination—for, otherwise, the mountain will never be climbed. That last 1,000 feet, 400 of which are obviously most dangerous for men in the weak state men must be at an altitude of 28,000 feet, will never be climbed by men who have been unduly exhausted by subsidiary efforts on the way up to that point. At all costs the final pair must be saved.

The donkey work on the North Col and in establishing the higher camps above the North Col must be done by members other than those upon whom the supreme call will be made. All are agreed, says Smythe, that economies on climbers' strength must be made on the slopes of the North Col. And these economies, both there and higher up, will have to be rigorously enforced if the mountain is to be climbed.

There are also other means of saving the final pair. The highest camp might be placed higher up. In 1933 the intention was to place it at 27,800 feet. Owing to the fierceness of the weather and the exhaustion of the porters it was not possible to carry it higher than 27,400. Even so, says Smythe, it was " a tremendous carry on the part of the porters, and it is very doubtful whether much more could be expected of them next time." Still, one does notice that in each successive expedition both porters and climbers *are* able to do more. The mountain has become more familiar to them. The men's spirit is raised by what has already been done. The art of acclimatization—that is, of adapting themselves to the new atmospheric conditions—has been better learned. It should, therefore, be possible to carry out Smythe's suggestion and place a camp on " a scree ledge near the base of the ' first step ' at about 27,800 feet."

This would be an improvement, but is it enough ? That is the question which constantly occurs to me as I read over the descriptions of these Everest climbs and talk with those who have made them. All these men are haunted by the reflection that they have not only to get to the top, but to get back. They must have time to get back ; and they must be in fit enough condition on the return to surmount the very serious difficulties on the way down. There is that awful 400 feet of couloir. Can men so enervated as they must be at 28,000 feet be expected to go up that gully and down it on the same day, as well as up and down that farther 600 feet to the summit ? It may be done if the climbers were reasonably fit, but it looks to me to be far too much to expect of men. And might not an alternative be considered which has been mentioned to me by one of the climbers? Might not a tremendous effort be made to establish a final camp on the final pyramid itself? Instead of expecting the final pair to do the whole 1,000 feet to the summit and back in one day, might not two days be made available for the effort—the first day being employed in ascending that dangerous 400 feet, and in establishing a camp at 28,400 feet, and the second day in climbing to the summit and returning at least to the 28,400 feet camp and, if possible, lower still?

It would be a lot to expect of the porters to carry a camp up the dangerous couloir to this enormous altitude. But by one method or another effort might be made to stimulate the spirit of a few specially selected porters to become very "tigers" of "tigers," and to surpass themselves in grandeur of achievement. For quite evidently more has to be expected of both porters and climbers than has yet been achieved. And by "saving" a final pair of porters as a final pair of climbers are to be saved, the thing might be done. Anyhow a severer call must be made or Everest will not be climbed.

Perhaps, too, the bodies, as well as the spirits, of both climbers and porters might be more highly stimulated on the next expedition. One very noteworthy experience of the last expedition was their craving for more food at great heights—and for more ordinary beef-steaky kind of food than the concentrated essence sort of food with which they were supplied. They were better acclimatized than their predecessors, and had heartier appetites. Perhaps the next expedition, still more familiar with the mountain, will have still heartier appetites. And if the organizers of the expedition can arrange for these ravenous appetites to be satisfied, for preparing more palatable meals, and generally for establishing the highest camps more comfortably and having vital stimulants—hot tea, or even water—ready when needed, great things might be done.

Through special efforts to stimulate the spirit of a few selected porters, and by arranging for plenty of appetizing food, and letting each climber have what suits him in particular, it might just be possible to establish a camp at 28,400 feet on the face of the final pyramid. And if by some superhuman effort that feat could be accomplished, then the climbers, and perhaps a porter, would set out for the summit freed of that haunting anxiety about ascending the 400 feet of dangerous couloir. They would be able to reach the summit well before noon, and have plenty of time to descend the couloir, get back on the main face of the mountain, and gain one or other of the high mountain camps before dark.

All this, however, though very pretty on paper, may be utterly impossible in practice. The weather may absolutely preclude it. For an assault on Everest ample time for the most deliberate and leisurely movements is required. Plenty of time is necessary for acclimatization, for the establishment and stocking of higher and higher camps. But this sufficiency of time is precisely what Everest weather does not allow. Even on a perfectly fine, cloudless day, out of the blue will come a raging tempest, driving the snow on the mountain in whirring swirls which may put a stop to operations for days. Then, ever in the background, is the monsoon.

The weather it is that decides. And in the weather the deciding factor is the precipitation of snow upon the steeply outward-facing slabs of rock on the approach to the final pyramid. The Everest climbers seem able to ride out the most terrific blizzards and to put up with the severest cold. But once even a sprinkling of snow has settled on the mountain they are brought to a standstill. The very fact that it is only a sprinkling constitutes the danger. Returning mountaineers, with little control of themselves and in the last stage of exhaustion, might be in the utmost peril on these outward-facing snow-sprinkled slabs.

This precipitation of snow is the decisive factor in the weather. When is it most likely to occur? It does not occur in the winter, for in that season the strong west winds are powerful enough to blow away the snow as fast as it falls. But there is a period of the year when these prevailing west winds diminish in power, and when the clouds coming up from the Indian side precipitate an increased amount of snow. The snow wins against the wind. Monsoon conditions have set in. On Kangchenjunga this may not greatly matter. On Everest it is decisive.

What, then, an Everest expedition has to determine is when these monsoon conditions may be expected to set in. And this cannot, of course, be done with any precision. But with the experience of five expeditions to guide them, an approximate estimate may be made. It may be assumed that the monsoon will begin to prevail at the earliest in the middle of May, and, at the latest, in the middle of June. Round about the first of June—a week or two on either side—the wind will weaken and the cloud increase. Snow will lay faster than it is swept away ; and the slabs will become too dangerous for climbers to venture on. This seems to be the rough conclusion to which climbers have come. And what a future expedition has to plan for is to reach the summit before this critical point is arrived at. They must be on the mountain while the wind is in the ascendant and before the snow has got the upper hand. It will be colder then. It will be vastly unpleasant. But it will be safer.

As to the chances of success, Ruttledge has said : "When we can synchronize four consecutive days of fine weather with the perfect simultaneous acclimatization and training of six men, perhaps two climbers will reach the summit."

This is a rather too nicely-calculated estimate, for it is quite certain that six perfectly trained and acclimatized climbers never will meet with *four* perfect days on Everest, and at that rate the mountain will never be climbed. But Ruttledge himself is sure it will be. So there must be a flaw somewhere.

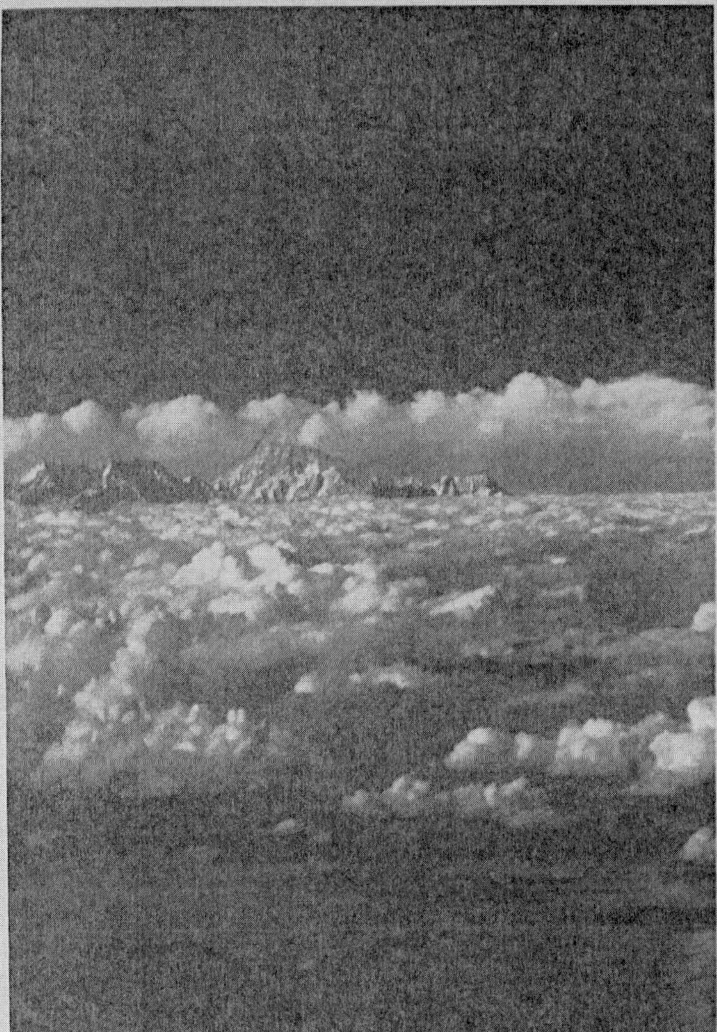

Photograph by the Everest Flight.

EVEREST ABOVE THE CLOUDS.

An infra-red photograph taken from a height of 22,800 feet and a distance of 105 miles.

Perhaps Bauer's words about the possibility of climbing Kangchenjunga—a mountain 800 feet lower but far more difficult—might be applied to Everest. If men attempt it at all, they must be optimists.

Anyhow, we onlookers at the mighty drama now being enacted cannot help rising to this optimistic note. We have seen the mountaineers overcome so many obstacles, and show such pertinacity and adaptability, that we are confident they will rise triumphant. We have been appalled at the ferocious malignity of the mountain, the devastating snowstorms, and the frightful cold. The operations have had to be more lengthy, and the mountain itself has proved more difficult than we had originally supposed. But we have been impressed by the resourcefulness of the mountaineers, by their ability to rise to the occasion and adapt themselves to severer conditions, and by the advance which they have made in mountaineering technique. We also note the improvement which has been made not only in the spirit but in the mountain-craft of the Himalayan porters. Everest has done something more than merely hurl back her assailants. She has stung them into developing their resources. She has called forth the unsuspected best within them.

All this makes us estimate the climbers more highly than they estimate themselves, and gives us confidence that even if Everest is only moderately lenient they will succeed.

CHAPTER VI

GERMAN EXPEDITIONS

Kangchenjunga, 1929, 1931

THOUGH, like the Everest expeditions, they ended in failure, the two Bavarian expeditions led by Dr. Paul Bauer in 1929 and 1931 to scale Kangchenjunga were exhibitions of mountaineering at its best. Enthralled by the attempts on Everest, these bold Munich mountaineers determined to attack Kangchenjunga. They were all trained mountaineers, and all had climbed together. They, therefore, formed a compact party of experienced climbers, able to secure the confidence of various German Alpine clubs and obtain from them five-eighths of their expenses, the remainder of which they had to pay for themselves.

Kangchenjunga is the very queen of mountains. The view of it from Darjiling is the finest in the world. No other can compete with it. From rich forests of oak and laurel and rhododendron, covered with ferns and orchids, and hung with graceful vines, we look down into a valley whose bottom is less than a thousand feet above sea-level, and then upward over ridge after ridge of forest-clad mountains to the snowy range whose summits are only forty miles away. All is veiled in a haze of purple, and as our eyes first light upon the highest summit we gasp with astonishment. Incredible, it seems, that earth could ever reach so near to heaven. For long we stare in silent wonder, taking slowly in the greatness of the scene. But, as we view it, never once does it enter our mind that any human being should presume to reach its summit. That looks far beyond the reach of any human being. Yet here were men who dared attain the unattainable. And they were no inexperienced enthusiasts like the ignorant young man who set out to climb Mount Everest by himself, whose body has just been recovered. They knew well, from their own adventures in the Alps, and from what they had read of Everest expeditions, what dangers they would have to face. Yet they deliberately faced the greatest. They dared to face the terrifying ridges, the dazzling ice-slopes, the fearsome avalanches, the biting cold, the blinding snowstorms, and the piercing winds of a mountain which is only 800 feet lower, and definitely more difficult, than Everest itself.

And they dared to attempt it in the monsoon. This, to those of us who had been accustomed to suppose that when the monsoon once broke mountaineering must cease, was the most surprising stroke of all. Yet this was the season deliberately chosen as the most suitable by Bauer. He arrived at Darjiling in the month of July—1929—in just the very season when rain descends in torrents day after day, when the mountain is hidden in mist, and when only for a few moments in the day is its summit seen—looking incredibly high through the mists.

Bauer's calculations were based on the assumption—which his subsequent experience proved to be true—that the time after the first burst of the monsoon, when the snow began to compact, would be the best season for the attempt. There might be much snow, but there would be less cold and less wind. Before and after the monsoon the high winds from Tibet would be too severe. So he made the bold decision to attack in the very middle of the monsoon.

The mountain he was going to attack was not a single upstanding peak. It is a mountain massif of five summits rising from a continuous ridge. The highest of these is 28,146 feet in height, and the lowest is 25,526 feet. It had previously been reconnoitred by competent mountaineers, notably by Freshfield, who had definitely concluded that the only way up was by the north-east spur leading on to the north-north-eastern ridge.

Such was the mountain which Bauer meant to attack. And in making his plans he was throughout assisted by members of the Himalayan Club, between whom and the Bavarians there sprang up a strong feeling of mountain camaraderie. Everest porters and other Sherpas and Bhutias were collected in advance. And through the rain-drenched forests of Sikkim, Bauer proceeded to his base at Green Lake Plain, on the Zemu Glacier, which flows down from the walls of Kangchenjunga.

From here he commenced a slow, methodical, most carefully-planned assault up the north-east spur. In his actions Bauer was bold. But in his boldest he was also careful. He was no slap-dash adventurer. Day by day, little by little, he hacked his way up the sharp-fluted ice-covered spur. Each step had to be cut. Sometimes tunnels had to be hewn through the ice. Camps had to be formed higher and higher up, and each camp gradually stocked with provisions. Often these camps were caves hacked out of the ice. It was no short brilliant assault he was making. It was a deliberate siege. It involved the most arduous work, and the most difficult porterage.

After careful preliminary reconnaissance of various ways to the summit Bauer had come quite definitely to the conclusion that the only possible way was by what came to be known as the north-eastern spur, which, higher up joining the ridge (or arête), led up to the summit. But even this north-eastern spur was most formidable. The upper part was clearly feasible. The feasibility of the lower part was by no means evident. Crowned by many verticle ice pinnacles, its aspect was terrible. Still, despite all appearances to the contrary, certain gullies, clefts, and ribs in the slopes of the pinnacles afforded some ground for hope that a way might be found, and Bauer decided to make the attempt. From the upper basin of the Zemu Glacier he would somehow or other force his way up the slope or wall, 2,800 feet in height, on to the more level portions of the crest of the spur.

The seventeen Sherpa and eight Bhutia porters were fitted out with clothes, boots, goggles, crampons, axes, and ropes, and the keenest of them were trained in axe and crampon work, rope management, and especially in the manner of belaying themselves. And on 26th August the first of three parties set out to establish Camp VI. at the foot of Kangchenjunga at a height of 16,183 feet. The first obstacle was an ice-fall, 700 feet in height, the way up which lay under threatening seracs and astride ice ridges as high as houses. This being overcome, Camp VII. was established at 17,749 feet, and from there effort after effort was made to reach the crest of the north-east spur. The steep slope leading up to the lowest depression in the crest was seamed with countless ice-flutings, between which arose sharp, serrated, and cornice-covered ribs. One effort after another failed. Two climbers, without loads and without porters, did indeed reach the crest by way of a steep ice gully, but the gully was too hard for the porters, and another way had to be found.

And here the resourcefulness of these Bavarian mountaineers came into evidence. They were not merely bold and courageous and pertinacious. They were men of resource. They initiated a new technique. They slowly forced a way up the slope to the crest by the arduous method of hewing breaches in the countless snow bosses. The first man, well belayed, would begin his heavy labour of cutting a way through these vertically rising hummocks. When he was exhausted another would take on the job. This was the method, but again and again they were forced by bad weather to return to Camp VII. or Camp VI. At last, on 13th September, the weather cleared, and two days of strenuous step-cutting in ice brought them at last to the crest of the north-east spur.

The scene was of "incomparable splendour." Nearly vertically below was the Twins Glacier, while slopes of sixty degrees led downwards to the Zemu Glacier. Shining icy pinnacles led upward to the summit of Kangchenjunga, while in a vast cirque about them towered many other great peaks. And down the icy slopes of these giants avalanches were perpetually thundering.

For two days they toiled at surmounting three ice towers on the level part of the ridge, and at last reached the base of a precipitous step. They could not overcome this in a day, and after belaying the porters to a well-buried axe, they proceeded to hack out of the ice a place on which a tiny tent could be pitched. In this Bauer and Biegel spent the night, while the others returned to Camp VII. Next day they started hacking out layer after layer of ice from the flanks of the first gendarme, till they could force a way past it and reach a *névé* slope at an angle of fully seventy degrees. In two hours they cut a good deep zigzag through it, then they enlarged a little ice crevice into a chimney. And by the early afternoon they were standing at the base of the last pinnacle separating them from the first platform. The following day, assisted by those who had come up again from Camp VII., they began cutting round the pinnacle. Eventually they established Camp VIII. on a little platform at an altitude of 20,737 feet.

Above this was the first perpendicular step. And now came the hardest labour of all. They had to hack their way through ice. The greater part of an overhanging cornice had to be flogged down. Then came a second and harder pinnacle, through which they drove a nearly vertical tunnel. Having overcome this obstacle, they had the dreadful piece of work of crawling up a wall of wind-blown powdery snow, all the time poised above the nearly perpendicular slope falling to the Twins Glacier.

Beyond that they came upon yet another pinnacle. They reached it on 23rd September. For two days they had to be working at the ice, burrowing a shaft perpendicularly upwards through a wide-stretching cornice. More fearful ice-work on the dizzy crest followed. Then an ice-cave was cut out to hold six to eight persons, in the interior of which, with the entrance made as small as possible, the temperature rarely fell below 25° F. And so Camp IX. was established at an altitude of 21,712 feet.

Above this Camp IX. there were no special difficulties. Camp X. was pitched on an easy and open terrain at 23,057 feet and an ice-cave scooped out. On 3rd October a reconnaissance was made to an altitude of 24,272 feet. The report was that no more difficulties were to be expected, but that, owing to snow conditions, a further camp would have to be pitched at

27,000 feet, and a final, Camp XII., at the base of the summit rocks.

The goal was at last in sight. But on 4th October forbidding black clouds appeared. By eight it was snowing hard. They waited all day for a clearance. None came. Nor on the next day. Nor on the day after. On 7th October they had definitely to abandon hope. At great risk, and with infinite difficulty, they fought their way back to Camp VI. And it was not until 12th October that they were back even there.

In 1931 Paul Bauer returned to the charge. The experience of Dyhrenfurth's expedition to Kangchenjunga in 1930 had confirmed him in the opinion that the north-east spur alone provided access to the summit. He therefore again attacked by that route, with five members of the previous expedition and four newcomers. But this time he arrived at the mountain earlier in the season. He was at the base by the middle of June, and on 14th July he began the assault of the terrible slopes. In consequence of this earlier arrival there was greater danger from avalanches, and if he had not already known the mountain he could hardly have climbed that first 2,000 feet leading on to the crest of the north-east spur. As it was, he had to have observation posts at the base on watch day and night, noting the direction and times of the ice and stone falls. And it was only due to these precautions that he was able to establish the old Camp VII., 18,569 feet.

Detachments worked daily, but only in the mornings up to about ten could they work in comparative safety. Even then, and on this highly-engineered track, they had to shelter behind vertical steps: and at the most dangerous points, where no such shelter was available, clamber over, or rush, one at a time, as quickly as possible. On two or three occasions the party descending from above was belated, and still on the march at midday. "Whistling, howling, thundering boulders, a cubic metre in size, flying downwards, would burst on impact into a thousand glass-like splinters. It was like being under hostile shell fire. Any one who could not keep absolutely cool, recognizing by the sound what was aimed for him and what was going wide, was lost indeed."

The danger was imminent, but Bauer makes some characteristic observations on it. "There was no sensible reason for it," he writes, "but on these occasions, though I invariably rose with stiffened limbs, I was not depressed by the danger—merely excited to the highest pitch of activity with a kind of wild joy in encountering these stone-falls. . . . It was just the wings of chance that enabled us to traverse these slopes so repeatedly without an accident. But it was not luck alone—the careful planning of the route, the meticulous care, the complete calm with which all encountered peril, had most to do with our escape. It was a triumph over the most treacherous danger which can threaten a mountaineer, that for months we could move about in safety in this stone-swept terrain."

Higher up the rocks were passed, and the climbers

had only snow and ice to deal with. The face had, from the distance, the appearance of fluted fish-bones. The climbers were confronted with fantastic, wondrous ice-formations—sprouting towers to a height of thirty feet — each one superimposed upon its neighbour. The labour of the ice-work was far greater than in the Alps. Many hundreds of cubic metres of snow and ice had to be hacked and scooped out of slopes inclined at an angle of fifty to sixty degrees.

The crest of the ridge was reached on 22nd July. But soon disaster came. Schaller was about to climb a gully in the ice. Quietly and cleanly he had enlarged each step. He had disappeared behind a snow-rib. Passang, an elderly, steady porter, had followed next, and had likewise disappeared behind the rib. The third man on the rope, Isin Norber, standing at the foot of the gully at a belay boulder, had paid out the rope, when all of a sudden Passang shot down the groove, followed immediately by Schaller, while masses of snow poured down the gully. Isin Norber, quick as lightning, doubled the rope, slinging it over the belay boulder. But the rope could not sustain the fearful shock of two falling bodies, and without a pause both continued falling, and vanished in the steep gully.

The bodies were subsequently found and laid to rest on a sunny rock islet. The climbers and porters then returned to the assault. They once more ascended to the crest of the ridge, and on 16th August were again at Camp VIII. In the beginning of September it snowed ceaselessly for five days, but they pressed on notwithstanding. Camp X. was established at 23,057 feet, and Camp XI. at 25,500 feet. The cold was now increasing, and they lived in ice-caves. On 17th September Hartman and Wien attained the steep snowy top of the great north-east spur at the point where it joins—or springs from—the north-north-east ridge leading to the summit. But here, at an altitude of 25,620 feet, they were brought to a standstill.

After sinking for about 200 feet the crest of the north-east spur abutted directly against a steep 400-feet slope forming the way of access to the main summit ridge. Owing to the condition of the snow the slope was now in a " truly shocking state." About a foot and a half of powdery snow lay lightly on the hard frozen lower strata.

On 18th September Allorein, Pircher, and Wien also reached this point and reported that " the slope forming the sole access to the summit ridge was at that moment totally unassailable owing to the great avalanche risks."

It was a cruel disappointment to have to turn back now the second time, after years of careful preparation, and after having slowly, methodically, with infinite care and patience overcome the many obstacles on the lower part of the mountain. For forty days, with hardly a rest, carrying heavy rucksacks and undergoing the severe strain of step-cutting in the ice, they had worked at an altitude of 18,000 feet and over. They had originated a new technique in coping with the peculiar difficulties presented by the ice formations. And now it seemed to Bauer that, once the wind had

Photograph by C. P. Skrine.

NANGA PARBAT FROM THE INDUS VALLEY.

cleared the snow away from the wall which confronted them, and the north-north-east ridge gained, the way to the summit would present no further technical difficulties. But the season was too late. He could not wait for the wind. He had to retire.

Bauer and his companions had failed to reach the summit. But whether it be in boldness, both of original conception and of execution, or in minute and methodical attention to detail, both in preparation and on the mountain, experts are agreed that as a mountaineering feat this assault on Kangchenjunga has never been excelled. Skill, courage, craftsmanship, mountain instinct, dogged determination, initiative and originality were all shown at their acme. And we like also to note that the good comradeship between these Bavarian climbers themselves was reciprocated by the Himalayan Club and the Himalayan porters. Kangchenjunga not only brought out the highest qualities of mind and body in each individual: it combined them all in the true fraternity of the mountains.

The Nanga Parbat Expedition, 1934

As an example of the perils which Bauer escaped, we may take the disaster which befell Merkl's expedition on Nanga Parbat in 1934—the greatest disaster which has ever occurred in the Himalaya.

Nanga Parbat is that most beautiful mountain at the back of Kashmir which stands out 10,000 feet above any other of its immediate neighbours, and 23,000 feet above the river Indus, which at its base cuts clean through the Himalaya on its way from Tibet to the Indian Ocean.

Merkl, who now for the second time attacked it, was a mountaineer of the first rank, and a leader who radiated confidence. By profession he had been an Inspector in the German State Railway Department, but at heart he was a mountaineer. He was a magnificent cragsman, and had accomplished many famous climbs. Also he had undertaken great ice-expeditions in the Swiss Alps, and had traversed the length of the Central Caucasus. And he was now thirty-four—the exactly right age for such an adventure.

On this second expedition to Nanga Parbat he took with him eight other mountaineers—all experienced and reliable men. In addition he had a cartographer, a geographer, and a geologist. For carrying loads on the mountain itself he employed thirty-five Sherpa and Bhutia porters trained in mountain-craft and discipline by the Everest and Kangchenjunga expeditions. And the whole was organized with the utmost thoroughness.

By 2nd May the whole party had assembled at Srinagar, the capital of Kashmir, and on 27th May the assault on the mountain began. For present purposes it is not necessary to describe this assault. Our object is to draw attention to the possibility of disaster, against which all Himalayan expeditions must be on their guard. By 4th July they had established Camp VII. at an altitude of 23,328 feet. The weather for days had been favourable—the mornings magnificent, at midday a brief mist, and splendid evenings. And when, on 6th July, Aschenbrenner and Schneider, with eleven porters, pushing on ahead of Merkl, Welzenbach, and Wieland to find a place for Camp VIII. came into full view of the summit they were filled with the joy of battle and confident that in four or five hours they would reach the summit, though it was still more than 2,000 feet above them.

And if they had been one day earlier—one day out of the forty which they had spent in the assault—they might have succeeded. And they might well have been earlier if they had not been delayed by burying a comrade who had died of pneumonia. But, as on Everest, literally out of the blue—out of the bluest sky—there arose a storm which, vastly increasing as daylight closed, became at night a raging hurricane. Camp VIII. had been pitched at a height of 24,650 feet. The large tent in which Merkl, Welzenbach, and Wieland lay was bent double by the terrible blasts, and the tent walls clattered unceasingly in the blizzard.

Thinking the storm would pass, the climbers kept their rucksacks ready packed for the assault on the summit next day. But on the morning of 7th July the storm raged so vehemently that hopes of starting that day had to be abandoned. "With maddened speed dense clouds of wind-driven snow raged over the plateau and hid the sun, so that it was quite dark at ten o'clock in the morning." Safe in their tents, climbers and porters did not suffer from the cold—bitter though it was. But the storm prevented the preparation of the simplest meals.

A second terrible night was passed in Camp VIII., and as the morning of 8th July brought no improvement it was agreed that the attempt to reach the summit must be abandoned, and Merkl gave orders for the descent to Camp IV. Aschenbrenner and Schneider, with three porters, were to go in advance and make a track through the very deep snow, while Merkl, Welzenbach, and Wieland, with the remaining porters, were to follow immediately. The storm was still raging; the utmost care, therefore, was necessary. Schneider went first, the three porters next, and Aschenbrenner brought up the rear, ready at any moment to arrest a fall. At one moment a porter was torn by the storm from the steps. It was only with the utmost difficulty that he was held on the rope and the whole party thus saved from destruction. As it was, the sleeping-bag was swept from his load, and it thus became necessary to reach Camp V. if they were not to be frozen. In the raging storm it was impossible to see more than ten or twelve yards ahead, so that many false tracks were made. To save the porters from making these exhausting tours, Aschenbrenner and Schneider unroped themselves from them opposite Camp VII. Telling the porters to follow immediately in their tracks, they proceeded downward and reached Camp VI. that evening, though completely exhausted and covered with ice from head to foot.

Meanwhile, the three porters got no farther than Camp VII., where they spent the night in the tent which had been left there. And Merkl, with the main party, did not get even as far as that. They had to bivouac that evening, 8th July, without a tent. One porter died, and in the morning Merkl's right hand, and both of Wieland's hands, were frost-bitten.

During the descent on 9th July Wieland died, only thirty yards from the tent of Camp VII. Three porters had to remain behind, partly through illness and partly through snow-blindness. Merkl and Welzenbach reached Camp VII. and remained there. Four porters descended farther, but owing to the severity of the storm could not reach Camp VI., and had to spend the night in a snow cave.

The storm continued on 10th July. Rescue parties frantically tried to ascend from Camp IV., but sank in the impassable snow. In the afternoon seven men were seen descending. They were porters. But only four, absolutely exhausted and with badly frost-bitten hands and feet, reached Camp IV. : the other three had died on the way.

On 12th July Aschenbrenner, Schneider, and Mülbritter, with three porters, succeeded in reaching Camp V. Their purpose was to force a track through the snow, and though they carried no loads, it was only after six hours' most arduous work that they succeeded in reaching Camp V., and a renewal of the storm drove them back to Camp IV., where they arrived completely exhausted.

Welzenbach died in Camp VII. during the night of 12th July.

On the morning of the 13th the last survivors, Merkl, with two porters, Gaylay and Angtsering, left Camp VII. for Camp VI., Merkl painfully supporting himself on two ice-axes. But his strength gave out before reaching the tent, and they had to build themselves into a small ice-cave. Beyond this Merkl could not move. The next morning Gaylay deliberately chose the heroic part of staying with his leader, and sent the younger porter, Angtsering, down the mountain. Those in Camp IV. saw a solitary figure appearing through the storm clouds. It was Angtsering. He had performed the amazing feat of finding his way by himself down the dangerous slopes, and fighting his way through storm and snow, had reached Camp IV. completely exhausted and terribly frost-bitten.

Desperate efforts were made by those below to reach the higher camps, but none were of any avail. Again and again they were engulfed in floods of freshly-fallen snow. Climbers and porters were utterly exhausted. All hope had to be abandoned. And Merkl and the faithful Gaylay must have perished on the 14th, or, at latest, the 15th of July, in the ice-cave at an altitude of at least 23,500 feet.

Of Merkl, his friend of twenty years, Berchtold, writes : " The mountains filled his life and made him the truest and most trusted of comrades. . . . On his last great adventure he was friend and leader in one. He never set his aim beyond what bodily fitness could endure, or technical ability achieve. He was methodical in preparation, and cautious in plan, but when committed he was grim in determination." Like a great leader, he remained with the last of his party to the last. And, true to their character, the Himalayan porters remained with their leader. Gaylay might have saved his life with Angtsering. He deliberately chose to die with his leader.

Disaster there was. Four Germans and six porters had lost their lives. But through the passing shadow of this direst of all Himalayan disasters shines the enduring light of manly comradeship—Merkl the German, and Gaylay the Sherpa, faithful to death—leader to porter, and porter to leader.

And the spirit of man remains undaunted. The Germans are even now planning a third expedition to Nanga Parbat, and Sherpa porters from Darjiling are volunteering to accompany them. Man means to win in the end.

CHAPTER VII

BRITISH EXPEDITIONS

Smythe on Kamet

SO far we have dealt only with failure and disaster met with by both Germans and British. But we have been concerned with the supreme peaks. Now we will examine adventures on peaks of a slightly lesser order of magnitude, and with successes on them. We shall see that while man is making his way higher and higher up the highest peaks he is at the same time reaching the summits of higher and higher peaks.

The most successful of these lesser expeditions was that led by Frank Smythe to the summit of Kamet, 25,645 feet. It is the first 25,000-feet peak to be conquered. And Smythe's expedition is a good, clear-cut example of what may be done by a small party of keen mountaineers acting on their own initiative. Forty years before his adventure, Conway had dared to hope of climbing a 25,000-feet peak. Now, what Conway had dreamed of Smythe had accomplished—but only been able to achieve because of what Conway himself had done in attracting the attention of mountaineers to the Himalaya, what Longstaff had done in climbing

Trisul, what the English climbers on Everest, and the German climbers on Kangchenjunga, had done in developing Himalayan mountaineering technique.

Collecting together a doctor from Oxford, a master from Harrow, a planter from East Africa, one officer from the Air Force and another from the Indian Army, he set-to organizing his expedition at Ranikhet in May 1930. Ranikhet is one of those heavenly "hill-stations" perched on the summit of the outer spurs of the Himalaya which afford such rest and refreshment to those from the sweltering plains of India who are fortunate enough to obtain leave to go there. It is about 7,000 feet above sea-level, and from it may be seen the broad plains of India on the one hand, and on the other the long line of snowy peaks which mark the high crests of the Himalaya. Nearly a hundred miles distant can be seen Kamet itself, 10,000 feet higher than Mont Blanc.

Smythe well knew what he had to reckon with in so audaciously venturing to scale one of the supreme heights. He had been with the German Dyhrenfurth expedition which had presumed to attack Kangchenjunga. Raymond Greene, the doctor from Oxford, Holdsworth the Harrow master, and Wing-Commander Beauman had not climbed in the Himalaya, and had only Alpine experience. Captain Birnie knew only lesser Himalayan heights, and Shipton only East African mountains. But all these companions of Smythe knew well from the tales of the Everest and Kangchenjunga expeditions what tackling one of the giants meant.

And it only increases our admiration of the human race to see men who are so fully aware of the dangers they will meet and the hardships they will have to endure, squarely and joyfully facing them, especially as no material reward is to be gained.

Nothing is more strenuous than climbing a Himalayan giant, and few things more dangerous. And no gold-mine or diamond-pocket is to be found on the summit. Far from making any money profit out of it, the climbers would be considerably out of pocket. Instead of being paid, they have to pay to do it. Yet they start as gaily as if they were out for the holiday of their lives. Which indeed they are. In their hearts they know that for the rest of their lives they will be able to look back upon this as the time in which they have best proved themselves men, and that they will have won for themselves the way to the esteem of those whose esteem they most care for.

But of themselves they could not do this deed. The assistance of the Himalayan people must be had—and of a few trained in the hard school of Everest. Everest porters must help them. So a few of these were brought from Darjiling, of whom the more noted were Lewa and Nima Tendrup.

Leaving Ranikhet on 18th May, the first few marches led through the beautiful outer ranges of the Himalaya. At times they would be down in a hot, enervating valley. More often they would be on the cool grass or forest-covered spurs of the snowy range. At Gwaldam, where is the last *dak* bungalow, they had a superb view of Trisul. From meadows bounded by forest they could look across an intervening ridge to the glorious snowy range. And, farther on, at the Kuari Pass, they had one of the greatest views in the whole Himalaya. They had expected much, but, as is usually the case in these mountains, the fact exceeded the expectation. They were dumb from sheer delight as they reached the summit of the Pass and looked out on that wonderful " other side." Arrayed before them in a mighty arc were great peaks of 23,000 and 25,000 feet in height, from Trisul on the right to the peaks of Kedarnath on the left. And straight before them was the peak they themselves had chosen to climb.

They were all men in the prime of life, aching to test their powers and prove their training, or they might well have been tempted to stay here and spend weeks in roaming along that ridge seeking finer view-points and feasting their souls on the infinite store of beauty about them. As it was, in their tense frame of mind they must undoubtedly have received an impression of mountain majesty which will lastingly affect them.

Having crossed the Pass, they pushed steadily on and, by 6th June, had finished the first stage of their enterprise and established their base camp, at an elevation of 15,500 feet, on the Raikana Glacier, one of the great glaciers running down from Kamet. From here they could see Kamet, though only the summit was visible as it appeared over an intervening ridge. But from this closer view they could observe that the north face, which they would have to ascend, was steep—

steeper than they had expected. They would not have a walk-over to the summit.

Smythe's intention was to proceed up the mountain by a series of stages, taking plenty of time so as to acclimatize the party to higher and higher altitudes. And before making his effort to reach the summit he aimed at establishing an Advanced Base Camp at an elevation of well over 20,000 feet, and, if possible, on Meade's Col, 23,500 feet. Relays of unequipped men were to work between Base Camp and Camp II., bringing up food. Then relays of equipped men would work between that and the Advanced Base until the latter had been fuelled and provisioned for at least a month. And all this time the actual climbers would be acclimatizing themselves. At Camp II. they would halt for some days before proceeding to Camp III., and at Camp III., which they eventually made the Advanced Base Camp, before proceeding to Camp IV. Acclimatization was to be put in the forefront of the programme.

They started on 8th June to establish Camp I. The sun was grillingly hot, and the snow on the Raikana Glacier soft. Turning a corner, they saw the East Kamet Glacier bounded by a mountain wall culminating in the Mana Peak, 23,862 feet. The angle of this wall was not Swiss but typically Himalayan. Owing to plasticity induced by temperature range, says Smythe, Himalayan ice can cling to rocks set at a terrifically steep angle. Had this wall been in the Alps, where, owing to a lesser temperature range, ice

By courtesy of Mr. John Murray.

DELICATE ARCHES OF SNOW SPANNING CREVASSES 150 TO 200 FEET DEEP.

is of a more brittle nature, there would have been few, if any, hanging glaciers adhering to the rocks. As it was, the precipices were crowned with walls of ice hundreds of feet thick.

The party passed now to the northern side of the East Kamet Glacier, and established Camp I. The next day they again experienced almost suffocating heat. There was also danger of avalanches of ice, for a block of ice weighing tons had been cast right across the glacier. The distance covered was only five miles, but it seemed interminable. They were rewarded by a full view of Kamet. The eastern precipice, nearly 7,000 feet in height, fell in one sweep from the summit to the East Kamet Glacier. But from the level plateau of Meade's Col slopes of snow and ice mounted to the summit, and these looked promising for an ascent. Camp II. was established by a block of rock with water close by in a hollow.

The 11th June was a day of rest, and as they were watching the Mana Peak, a few miles south of Kamet, a mass of ice on the lower slopes collapsed and fell from the edge of a hanging glacier. This set falling a larger piece, the size of a cathedral, which slowly leant away from its parent glacier and "with deliberate yet irresistible force, and with the stateliness of a felled factory chimney, toppled on to the slope below and rent into a million fragments."

After a day's reconnaissance they established Camp III., which they had had eventually to make the Advanced Base Camp, in a snowy valley 200 feet below the crest of the ridge. It was a hard day's work; they had to make their way up a gully filled with soft snow. Increasing shortness of breath necessitated frequent halts, and higher up a biting wind arose. The next day porters took six hours to make the ascent. The wind again arose, and a blizzard blew on the camp.

One of the peculiarities of the Himalaya noted by Smythe is that the mountain-sides invariably prove to be steeper than they look. This optical delusion may be produced partly by the vast scale on which the peaks are built and partly by the unusually clear atmosphere. From Camp III. the rock and the precipice leading on to the ridge had appeared moderately steep. When they came actually to climb it next day on a preliminary reconnaissance, it become more formidable every moment. And their lack of acclimatization was made apparent by their breathlessness.

On 16th June they set out again to find a way to a site for Camp IV. The main couloir up which they had expected to find a way had proved to be far too dangerous. They now had to seek a new route. It was a difficult and a dangerous business, and they had a gruelling day's work. They had to climb steep snow-slopes, to cut steps in ice, to clamber up rocks, to drive pitons in the rock and fix ropes as a help for the porters in traversing dangerous parts. But at last they succeeded in making a route, and once more returned to Camp III. On 17th June they continued the work of forcing a way to the site for Camp IV. and cutting steps on the final ice-slope.

On 20th June Smythe started to reconnoitre a site for Camp V. on or near Meade's Col, at an altitude of 23,300 feet. They proceeded over a snow-slope, hard at first but soon melting under the fierce rays of the sun. It became softer and softer, and they sank in over the top of their boots. Farther on they had to cut steps in an ice-wall when altitude, a blazing sun, and the soft snow had so sapped their energy that a few swings of the axe set the heart galloping and lungs gasping. They fixed on a site a little below Meade's Col. And now, for the first time, they had a full and close view of the uppermost slopes of Kamet.

They had fully intended to have placed another camp higher still before striking for the summit ; but they were now unexpectedly fit and well-acclimatized, and the weather was perfect, so they decided to risk something and make an attempt to reach the summit in one day direct from this Camp V. And after the decision was made they felt strangely happy and confident. It was a bold stroke, and it swept overboard their ideal scheme of proceeding by steady stages and not allowing themselves to be deflected from their plans by any fine weather. But it succeeded.

At 8 a.m. they left the camp, knowing that they would not only have to reach the summit but return to their camp before nightfall. And that return journey might be the most dangerous part of the whole venture, for exhausted men are not always as careful as they should be about looking after each step they take.

For the first thousand feet the going was not difficult, it was merely exhausting: it lay through deep snow. Afterwards the mountain became both difficult and dangerous. Just beneath the snow was ice. Steps had to be cut. Energy for cutting steps was hard to find. And though exhausted and listless, and in a general state of not caring much what happened to them, they had yet to take very much care indeed, for they were on the knife edge of a ridge, and a slip would carry them slithering over ice and precipice on to the glacier thousands of feet below. They ascended very slowly, making little more than 200 feet an hour. It took them seven and a half hours to climb the final 1,500 feet. And it was not till 4.30 that they at last threw themselves flat on the summit, utterly exhausted.

But on a Himalayan summit there can be no rest and no relaxation. The moment the summit has been won a retreat must be made or the climbers may be benighted on their return. And Smythe and his companions were very late. They had to descend 2,300 feet of dangerous snow and ice before they would be in safety. Smythe was, however, well aware of the danger before him and how he would cope with it. He would allow no laxity. The climbers, with long lengths of rope between them so that a slip might be retrieved, proceeded cautiously downward, and just as dark set in reached their camp in safety.

Smythe's conquest of Kamet is a magnificent example of the value of having a well-thought-out plan beforehand and then throwing it to the winds when necessity should arise. According to theory he should have sternly resisted every temptation of fine weather and near sight of the summit, and have plodded methodically on, piling up his stores, establishing one further camp on the mountain face itself, and steadily letting acclimatization work out its beneficial result. Instead, he gave his plans the go-by. He saw his opportunity; he seized it. He went for the top, and he got there.

But, as the Duke of Wellington said of the Battle of Waterloo, "it was a damned close-run thing." He got back to camp only just in time. He ran things very fine. He might have been benighted on the ice-slopes of the mountain, and a night there in their exhausted condition might have had fatal consequences. Moreover, those who would wish to imitate Smythe's boldness should note that in the very moment of victory he did not allow his vigilance to sleep for an instant. He did not allow either exhaustion or elation to keep him from carefully watching each step he took on the way down those dangerous slopes. With all his boldness he yet kept himself sternly in hand. Thereby he not only won his victory: he preserved it.

Oliver on Trisul

A less ambitious enterprise, but valuable as showing what can be done at small expense by a subaltern serving in India during his leave, was that to the Kumaon Himalaya led by Lieutenant P. R. Oliver, who had with him Mr. David Campbell, a nephew of

General Bruce, and was able to benefit by the advice from that veteran Himalayan mountaineer.

Their rough intention was to climb a 23,000-feet peak which was fairly accessible and which had not already been climbed. Their choice had finally fallen on Dunagiri, which is 23,184 feet, and is situated in that wonderful region at the back of Kumaon which is dominated by the great peaks Kamet and Nanda Devi—Dunagiri itself being one of the minor peaks on the ridge which bounds what is called the Nanda Devi basin.

They started from Ranikhet on May 11, 1933, and on the next day, from the Forest Rest-house at Gwaldam, they had the famous view of Trisul, 23,560 feet, first climbed by Longstaff. In the early morning the primrose-tinted snows were just catching the slanting rays of the rising sun, and the mountain-top appeared radiant above hills and valley still lost in night. Four days' marching, during which they passed over a beautiful wooded ridge, brought them to the valley of the upper Ganges along which lies the pilgrim-route to Badrinath. Many pilgrims they met here, mostly weak and ailing, with no eye for the beauty of the gorge-like valley, and very different from the robust and cheerful Kesar Singh, who had climbed with Smythe on Kamet, and who here joined them and was to .prove a tower of strength. Proceeding, they reached Joshimath, where two branches of the Ganges meet, and opposite which, above deep gorges, tower rock-peaks of terrific aspect backed by savage shapes of ice and snow.

From Joshimath they marched up the Dhauli branch of the Ganges to Tapoban on 19th May, and on the next day to Suraintota, from whence they had their first sight of Dunagiri. There they ascended the Tolma stream to Tolma. Beyond this the hillsides were very steep, with nearly impassable areas of bamboo alternated with wildernesses of thorn. At Shem, which they reached on 24th May, they formed a base camp for their operations on Dunagiri, but they soon found that the chances of even moderate success on this particular peak were very few. To tackle it they would need a larger and better-equipped party. They therefore gave up all idea of climbing it and turned their thoughts to Trisul. This would not have the interest of Dunagiri, which was a virgin peak, whereas Trisul had already been climbed by Longstaff. But it was, anyhow, a 23,000-feet peak, and Oliver determined to climb it, though he would have to work alone, as Campbell had to return to England.

On 10th June Oliver set off on his adventure. His first march took him to Utui, a lovely sheltered alp on the north slopes of the ridge which bounds the Nanda Devi basin. In shape this basin is like a gigantic horse-shoe with the open end narrowed to a neck through which flows the Rishi Ganga, one of the main con-tributaries of the Ganges. The whole basin may be regarded as one of the remote sanctuaries of the Hima-laya, to which only a few hardy hillmen penetrate with their flocks in search of pasturage. But there is an inner sanctuary of this sanctuary, which no one yet had entered. It is formed by a ridge cutting across the centre space of the horse-shoe, and it is only breached by a narrow gorge through which thunders the Rishi Ganga. At the time of Oliver's visit this gorge was thought to be impassable. But in the following year, 1934—as will be presently described—it was daringly explored by Shipton, the Everest climber.

On 11th June Oliver continued his climb up the outside rim of the Nanda Devi basin, making his way through thick forest and undergrowth. In three and a half hours he reached the open alp of Lata Kharak, and from there crossed the ridge at about 13,000 feet and looked down into the Nanda Devi basin itself. There followed an hour and a half of coasting along the huge precipices which fall into the Rishi Ganga, and then they reached a bivouac, called Yeru Thela, in the bed of a steep gully. The next day's march lay at first along precipices, then up an enormous rock gully which led up to a little col overlooking the broad Durashi grazing grounds, to which they now descended.

Next day they climbed the eastern rim of the Durashi bowl. The scene ahead was magnificent. It must have been one of the great sights of the whole Himalaya, for facing them, and only twelve miles distant, was the great peak Nanda Devi, 25,645 feet, which extends right into the centre of the basin. Of this we shall hear more from Shipton later on. Meanwhile, Oliver descended to his next camp, Dibrugheta, an oasis of brilliant green between the brown slopes above and the dark forest below. A six hours' march on 14th June led them over a wooded shoulder and down to Duti, which is situated in thick scrub about three-quarters of a mile below the junction of the Rishi and Trisuli Nalas. A day had to be spent in cutting trees with which to bridge the Rishi Ganga torrent. That river safely crossed, they ascended the valley of the Trisuli stream and pitched camp about a mile short of the moraines of the Batatoli Glacier.

Passing the site of Longstaff's "Juniper Camp" on 16th June, they climbed along the boulder-strewn hill-sides until they reached the end of the true left moraine of the Trisuli Glacier, and finally pitched their Base Camp at an altitude of 14,300 feet on a flat place near a stream, in the trough between the moraine and the mountain-side. From here Oliver sent down most of the unequipped men to Juniper Camp, while he himself, with the better equipped and trained porters, prepared for his attack on Trisul itself.

The prospect of reaching the summit was not hopeful. During the preceding days the weather had steadily been getting worse. Rain had fallen nearly every night, and even the early mornings had not been clear. During the night of 17th June snow fell at the Base Camp. But Oliver got on the move the next day and pitched Camp I. on a ridge leading up to the North Ridge of Trisul, and about 1,000 feet above the moraine of the Trisuli Glacier. He was now planted actually on the mountain itself at an elevation of about 17,500 feet.

At 7.40 a.m. on 19th June he and his seven high-camp porters started up the mountain and, ploughing their way through snow slopes, pitched Camp II. on a fairly level place on the broad ascending ridge. It was a glorious day, and the view was of that astounding mountain brightness which makes everything appear as if it had been revealed for the first time. The dominant feature in the scene was, of course, Nanda Devi, with its double turreted mountain ridge. The higher summit—the western—was like the Cenotaph in shape, and was a veritable monument of mountain inaccessibility. It was twelve miles distant ; and, far away, could be seen Kamet, climbed by Smythe two years before.

Snow fell gently on the 20th, and Oliver rested in his Camp II., vainly expecting the return of three porters whom he had sent down on the previous evening to Camp I. to bring up another tent and more food, and so enable him to establish a third camp higher up, and from there make his final effort. The porters did not appear on the 20th, but Oliver assumed that they would anyhow arrive on the 21st and pitch the reserve tent at Camp II. So at 7.45 a.m. on the 21st he and the remaining four porters started up the mountain, taking two tents with them. The weather was clear up to about 22,000 feet. Above that all was in cloud. The outlook was not promising, and as they could see no signs of the three porters returning to Camp II., Oliver hesitated between returning to Camp II. and establishing a Camp III., which latter course would mean that the four porters would have insufficient food. Kesar Singh then suggested a third course—the bold one of making a dash straight away for the top. Oliver and he were to make this bid for victory, while the other three were to put up the tents to shelter themselves from the fierce wind which had now sprung up, and to have hot drinks ready for Oliver and Kesar Singh on their return. A correct mountaineer would scarcely have made so rash a decision. For it was now 11.15 a.m., they were 2,500 feet from the summit, and the summit was hid in cloud.

But Oliver accepted the suggestion, and at 11.30 he and Kesar Singh, as lightly laden as possible, set forth, ploughing diagonally up the snow slopes leading to the summit ridge. It was fatiguing work, as often the snow crust would give way and they would be plunged into a foot or more of soft snow. They would have liked to rest now and then, but time was short and, except for brief panting intervals every thirty or forty paces when they would double up over their ice-axes, they had to plod on. In occasional bright intervals they would see perhaps a couple of hundred yards ahead, but for the most part they were enveloped in cloud. It seemed as if they would never reach the top. Oliver determined to keep on till three o'clock, beyond which time it would not be safe to go, as he must leave enough time for the return journey. But he says that "determined" is hardly the right word to use, for it implies inflexibility of purpose, whereas he had none, and merely moved along with a kind of angry doggedness.

At about one o'clock they reached the summit

ridge and turned left along it. At 2.30 they arrived on a little plateau which they thought must be the top. They accordingly flopped down and shook hands. But a bright interval showed a short continuation of the ridge to a higher bump. They crawled up this, and at 2.45 they found themselves on the real summit. Again they shook hands and felt pleased—though only mildly pleased, for, like the Everest climbers, they were too exhausted to feel anything strongly.

Alas ! they had no view. They were in the very heart of the Himalaya, 23,560 feet above sea-level : but all they saw was bleak whiteness. This would seem unsatisfying. Yet, after all, Oliver had not gone there for the view. Better views may be had at far less cost from a much lower level. The view from Darjiling, for example, can be had for the price of a railway ticket. Oliver had gone there to test his manhood against the mountain. His physique, his determination, his judgment, his skill had all been tried and found sufficient. His manhood had been proved, and he could ever after be proud of the result.

They rested only seven minutes on the summit, and then hurried down, for visibility was bad and snow was falling. They were horrified to find how weak they were. They had no strength to keep their balance on the unevenly crusted snow, and staggered like drunken men. Kesar Singh, who had been weakened by carrying a load earlier in the day, showed an extraordinary lack of control in his movements. He fell several times. Worse still, he suddenly said he could not see properly. The wind was blowing with great spite, and ice crusted on their eyebrows and lips. Oliver felt thoroughly frightened. All he could do was to drive Kesar on in front of him, ordering which way to take. Gradually the weather got clearer as they descended, and at 4.30 they were back where they had left the porters. They then struck camp, and at 5 were on their way down the mountain again, Oliver himself shouldering a ten-pound load. At last, at 7.30, just as darkness was falling, they reached Camp I.

The next morning, in a dismal flurry of snow, later becoming sleet and rain, they descended to the Base Camp. Through mist and rain the whole party then made their way back across the Nanda Devi basin. At Durashi they met herdsmen with sheep and goats, and on 27th June they arrived back at Tapoban. Here Oliver parted from his cheery Bhutia porters, and on the 28th started for Ranikhet.

It was a great little enterprise, most nobly carried through by Englishman and Bhutia alike. Oliver had not achieved his ambition by climbing a virgin 23,000-feet peak, but he had climbed one which had been climbed only once before. He had gained experience, he had shown his mettle, and maybe there are higher things yet in store for him on Everest.

Shipton in the Nanda Devi basin

Next year, 1934, a similar small expedition was led by Eric Shipton into the same Nanda Devi region.

Shipton was one of those who, in 1933, had reached the 28,000-feet level on Everest. But on this occasion his object was not to climb Nanda Devi or any other big peak, it was to penetrate to the inmost sanctuary of this most marvellous basin dominated by the mighty Nanda Devi. No one hitherto—not even a shepherd of those parts—had been able to force his way through the terrific gorges to it. Longstaff and Oliver had only climbed in the outer precincts. So Shipton, on the advice of Longstaff and Ruttledge, determined to make the attempt to follow up the Rishi Ganga to its source at the base of the Nanda Devi.

Eric Shipton took with him H. W. Tilman, with whom he had climbed in Eastern and Central Africa. As porters they had two Everest Bhutia porters, Angtharkay and Passang ; and a third, Kusang Nangir, a man of extraordinary toughness and imperturbability. This party reached Ranikhet on May 9, 1934, engaged local porters for the march across the Kuari Pass to Joshimath, and left on the 11th. For nine delightful days they marched through the lovely foothills of the range, and crossed passes clothed with pine, oak, and rhododendron woods. And from the Kuari Pass they had that view of the great peaks for which the Pass is so famous.

Joshimath was reached on 19th May, and on the 22nd they left again, and passing through Surai Tota, struggled over the ramparts of the Nanda Devi basin and looked down an 8,000 feet precipice into what they thought must be one of the most fantastic gorges in the world. Only just visible in depths below, yet sending up a roar like Niagara, was the Rishi Ganga. They kept along the northern flanks of the valley until a mile or so beyond the junction of the Trisuli stream, then bridged the river and crossed on to the southern bank, till on 28th May, in a heavy snowstorm, they reached the point where the Rhamani stream flows into the Rishi Ganga from the north, and here they established their base at an altitude of about 11,800 feet.

Now came the problem of how to force their way through the gorge into the inmost sanctuary four miles distant. The cliffs of the northern side looked utterly impregnable, rising straight out of the river-bed and culminating in peaks of over 20,000 feet above sea-level. And the grim, relentless cliffs on the southern side looked nearly as impracticable : the chances of finding a continuous route along their precipitous sides seemed very slender indeed. Yet there was just a chance. And after an exhaustive search among a number of freak rock formations they succeeded in effecting a passage. They made a series of delicate traverses over giddy drops into the river a thousand feet below ; and by roping up the more difficult sections and carrying the loads among them in relays, they were able to reach a point half a mile from the end of the gorge. Here the difficulties became so great that they were driven to descend to the river-bed. Along this they did indeed, after some perilous crossings of the river, find their way. But it was wholly impossible to take loads along it. They had therefore to search again for a route along the face of the southern cliffs ; and careful search revealed a continuation of their route 2,000 feet above the river on the southern side. And on 6th June, after nine days' work, they established an advanced base at 13,000 feet, in the inner sanctuary of the Nanda Devi basin.

Shipton describes it as an extraordinary freak of nature. It is enclosed by a gigantic rampart of scores of peaks between 20,000 and 23,000 feet in height. The only breach in this rampart is the gorge through which he had just come. In the centre rises one of the most colossal masses of rock in the world, the majestic peak of Nanda Devi, the sides of which are so exceedingly steep that even the plastic Himalayan ice can find little on which to cling. And north and south of the peak flow two great glaciers which form the source of the Rishi Ganga.

The interior of the basin was surprisingly beautiful. Instead of grey moraines, as Shipton had expected, there were extensive areas of rich pasturage, gay with flowers. Lakes also were there, on whose deep blue and green surfaces were reflected the icy crests of the great peaks. And the large herds of mountain sheep and goats were so tame that they only regarded the strange new visitors to their country with curiosity.

The northern part of this sanctuary Shipton and Tilman now investigated and surveyed. From a lateral valley they were able to see to fullest advantage the colossal northern face of the twin peaks of Nanda Devi. From the summit ridge it falls in one unbroken sweep to the glacier at its foot. For hours on end, in every combination of light and shadow, they were able to gaze upon that cirque without ever getting tired or losing their early amazement at the sight.

They made several climbs on to the rim. Shipton reached a 20,000-feet col, and from it climbed a peak of about 21,000 feet. And they made two attempts to climb peak 119, which is nearly 23,000 feet. But on both occasions they failed on account of dangerous snow conditions. On 24th June the monsoon broke—a good fortnight before they had expected it—and they had to retreat from the sanctuary and spend the next two months mountaineering and exploring in the region round the Gangotri source of the Ganges. But at the beginning of September they returned to Nanda Devi. By a lucky chance none of the vital points of the traverse along the dangerous southern cliffs of the gorge had been seriously altered by landslips, and on 8th September they were again in the sanctuary. The weather was now continuously fine, and they were able to work at their survey of the southern section without interruption.

The highest peak on the rim here is 22,320 feet, and Shipton named it Maiktoli, after the grazing ground on the south side of it. On 11th September Shipton and Tilman set out to climb it, but Tilman became unwell, and Shipton went on with Angtharkay and Kusang. A camp was established at about 20,000 feet, and on 12th September, in face of a wind of almost Everest severity, they reached the summit. All the way up and from the summit they had views of surpassing grandeur, and even the great southern face of Nanda Devi seemed to be dwarfed by the mere extent of the panorama.

For a few days more they climbed about on the rim, then they returned homeward. Their " five crowded months amongst some of the most glorious mountains in the world " had been for them a " season of supreme happiness."

Marco Palis in Kumaon and Spiti

An expedition of a yet different kind was that led by Mr. Marco Palis to the Himalaya in 1933. Neither he nor his companions, Mr. F. E. Hicks, Mr. C. F. Kirkus, Mr. R. G. Nicholson, and Dr. Charles Warren had been near the Himalaya before. They had lived their lives in England. But at times they had climbed together and camped together in the Alps as well as in England. And now they would have the adventure of their lives in the Himalaya. They did not aspire to climbing any of the greater peaks. But they did wish to explore some noble group of peaks, and perhaps climb one or two of the lesser giants. And they, like Oliver, selected the region at the sources of the Ganges as their field of adventure.

They sailed from England on April 1, 1933, for Calcutta, spent a week in Mussouri collecting coolies, and from there set forth on 10th May—as it happened, just the day before Oliver was leaving Rhanikhet in the same general direction.

Harsil was reached in eight marches. "Not a moment passed but it was full of delights. Immense thickets of white rose scented the air for miles. There were lovely pink magnolias . . . and in the centre of a village green there stood a brilliant orange tree covered with plume-like spikes of flowers. . . . The stage before Gugmani lay through the most glorious woods, with deep wine-red rhododendrons and fresh green bamboos, underneath which was a carpet of white pæonies." Here at Harsil the cheery Mussouri coolies were paid off, and four permanent porters for the glacier region ahead were engaged ; for from Harsil onward there would be sterner work to do.

The chief of the four was Ishwar Singh, who proved himself to be intelligent, open-minded, scrupulously honest, devoted, and humane. In addition, he had remarkable tact with every sort of person whatever his rank or race.

At Gangotri temple the path ended, and at Gaumukh (the cow's mouth), where the Ganges issues from a glacier, the local men were discharged, and only Jadhs (Bhutias) and Tibetans taken on.

The expedition had now before them group after group of peaks of the 20,000-feet order of magnitude on which to test their mettle. There were none of the supreme giants of the Himalaya, such as are found in Nepal. Nevertheless, they were well above the Alpine order to which the climbers had hitherto been accustomed, and they eagerly set to conquer them. They began with "a small subsidiary peak about 18,000 feet high." Then they attacked the Kedarnath group, and climbed their first 20,000-feet peak. Then followed "a snowy peak about 20,400 feet high." Then they reached an altitude of about 21,600 feet on "a big white mountain," but were forced by a heavy snow-storm to turn back when within 500 feet of the summit. A rocky peak then tempted them, but some little distance below the summit they were held up by smooth, holdless slab-rock which was periodically swept by vicious little avalanches. They were successful, however, in climbing a peak (about 20,600 feet) in the Kedarnath group. Then followed their highest achievement. On 18th June Kirkus and Warren climbed the central Satopanth peak (22,060 feet).

This feat they accomplished by successive stages. They pitched Camp II. at 19,500 feet on the col at the foot of the final peak, and from it had an "incredible view of the great west face of the mountain falling almost vertically for 3,000 feet." There followed a gruelling day. To avoid a 500-feet step they had to make a long and trying traverse across rotten rock and snow, and then return to the ridge across a dangerous-looking slope of snow and stones. On the ridge itself the climbing became definitely difficult, and the rocks terribly loose. Eventually they pitched Camp III. at 20,900 feet, on an inadequate snow-patch overhung by great cliffs. That night they experienced another snow-storm, and began to despair of reaching the summit. However, by nine o'clock on the following morning the weather cleared, and they set out for the summit.

Immediately before them rose an appalling tower about 100 feet up, the upper section of which was covered with rocks, loose and cold, and mantled with fresh snow. It was technically very difficult, and caused the climbers much uneasiness—even fright—before they succeeded in surmounting it. They rested for a time, made some tea, and then started to tackle the summit, which they had seen through the clouds quite close. They followed up an easy snow ridge, corniced on the right and falling steeply on both sides, and soon after one o'clock reached the summit, 22,060 feet above sea-level.

They had achieved their ambition. They had conquered a 22,000-feet peak. But by bad luck they were enveloped in cloud. So they stayed only a few minutes, and then descended to camp at 21,700 feet.

The descent on the following day was full of difficulty. The monsoon had evidently started, and when they had to leave the ridge to traverse the side, small snow avalanches and boulders were crashing down in an alarming manner. They reached the col at 19,500 feet very tired, for they had been moving roped together, one at a time, for the past three days. But even now their difficulties and dangers were not at an end, for once more it snowed all night. Warren was partially snow-blind. Food was almost exhausted. And they began to fear lest they might be marooned on the mountain. However, in spite of the snowstorm they were finally able to reach the Base Camp.

The monsoon having definitely set in, the whole

expedition moved to the old birchwood camp below Gaumukh. The wood was now in full leaf, and the many flowers, including a species of fragrant daphne, were a welcome change from the rocks and ice and grey skies of the glacier region.

Proceeding farther downward they had great difficulty in reaching Gangotri. At first the way led through grand forests with rich undergrowth of white roses and banks of white lilies. Then came a most formidable obstacle : huge cliffs, very smooth in their lower portion, overhanging the raging, swirling river, and, higher up, a not much more promising rock-face. Fortunately in the middle were a number of cracks and ledges ; and along these the climbers, aided by rose bushes and juniper roots, found a way. The porters then divided the loads into small portions, and astonishing the Englishmen by their agility, even with loads on their backs, managed, by making a succession of journeys, to get the whole outfit across the dangerous obstacle.

Next day they passed Gangotri, and the day after were back in Harsil. Here they rested for a few days, giving themselves complete relaxation and enjoying an abundance of fresh food. But Hicks and Kirkus had to return to England as their holiday time was expiring, and the other three prepared for the second part of their programme, the exploration of the monsoon-free Spiti region.

This remote region they would reach by way of the Nela Pass. Leaving Harsil on 11th July, they marched through a magnificent deodar forest with an undergrowth of syringa, now in full bloom and sweetly scenting the air. The first camp was pitched in a glade of magical beauty, carpeted with tall-growing strawberry plants and shaded by ancient birch trees. The second march was largely over meadows and across drifts of old snow, and partly through birch woods. Open coombes of rich pasture, true "alps," were also crossed. And the party encamped in a meadow on the hillside, surrounding which they found flowers in great variety—mauve irises, potentillas, both yellow and orange and dark crimson, pale orange lilies, a mauve meconopsis poppy with a yellow centre, and bushes of white rhododendrons.

The next march was equally beautiful, and they encamped at Khyarkuti, a meeting-place of several deep glens, each affording a glimpse into a fine glacier-coombe with its dominating peaks. This, says Palis, would be an ideal spot for a base camp, since it lacks nothing a man requires. And by "a man" we must presume he means a mountaineer of simple needs. It is sheltered. Fuel is abundant. Sheep and milk can be had from the shepherds. It is easily accessible from Harsil, so that supplies and transport present no problem. The scenery is magnificent, and the mountain slopes are covered with flowers, small pale lemon-yellow rhododendrons, huge purple auriculas, three species of fritillaria (green, white, and pink), while primulas grow in the marshy places, and kingcups where the snow has only just melted.

Then there are asters and sheets of big white anemones with many blooms on a stalk. Palis could imagine no better scene for the operations of a lightly-equipped party who did not mind their peaks not being especially lofty—that is, not much over 20,000 feet.

They rested at this lovely spot an extra day, and then started for the Nela Pass. The Pass itself is reached by a tedious march up a not very steep glacier. It is about 18,000 feet high, and the view from the top is undistinguished. Descending, they reached the village of Chitkul at the limit of trees, where they found several specimens of blue poppy, great purple banks of willow herb, and a small dark rhododendron. Here they were welcomed by an assemblage of village elders, and they found the village itself architecturally interesting, for the houses were adorned with admirable wood-carving on doors, rails, and open verandas. Another day's march brought them to Sangha, and they were now in the valley of the upper Sutlej, the great river which, rising in Tibet, cuts clean through the Himalaya and descends into the plains of the Punjab. They proceeded to Chini, on the Hindustan–Tibet road, and thence to Poo, which they left on 30th July for Namgya, from whence they got their first sight of the peak Leo Pargial, 22,210 feet, which was one object of their ambitions when they left England.

Below Namgya, they crossed the Sutlej by a bridge, and mounted a dreary hillside—and in Spiti the hillsides *are* dreary—to Tashigang, and thence on to Nako in the Spiti valley. Nako is a green oasis in the general drabness, and is about 12,000 feet above sea-level. But if the country was dull the people were "most friendly and helpful, and seemed to possess a lively sense of humour." They were Tibetan in character, and in the village were many prayer-wheels and chortens.

The weather was still grey when they set out to climb the peak. They halted that evening at the upper limit of fir wood. The next day the way still lay over desolate mountain-side with vast scree slopes, ridges of crumbling rocks, and moraines. They made several reconnaissances, and on account of mist had trouble in deciding which route to the summit they should take. Eventually they fixed on a col between the north or highest peak, and a smaller rock mountain, and on this col they pitched their third camp.

From it they could see their route would be up a vast snow-face till they reached a broad shoulder of the mountain, whence a sharply-defined ridge led to the summit. All seemed plain sailing; but in the night a fierce blizzard arose, and their spirits fell. In the afternoon, however, the weather cleared, and Palis and Warren packed up their light tent and, with some provisions, set out up the mountain, and that evening anchored their tent on an ice-platform. The next morning, 10th August, they made for the top. Instead of ice they now found all snow. The day was brilliant, and they were full of hope. But after they had made a short halt and brewed some tea, clouds began to gather rapidly. Feature after feature became blotted out. A chilly wind began to blow. The ice-axes sizzled ominously. Their hair stood on end and crackled in harmony. Violent peals of thunder shook the mountain, and it was clear that a nasty storm was brewing. But there were lulls, and in the lulls they pressed on bit by bit. At 2.30 the storm seemed to abate. Then some rocks appeared out of the mist. They made a final effort—and were on the summit. Leo Pargial, 22,210 feet, had been conquered.

Alas ! from this peak, as from the other, there was no view. All was hidden in cloud. And they could not wait for the clouds to disperse. They had to hurry down. White woolly mist shrouded them all the way, and a violent storm of wind and hail made no impression on it. By six they were back in their tent on the western col. During the night the storm came on again, and the next morning the whole mountain was covered with new snow. It was evident that they had, at great risk, climbed the mountain on the last feasible day.

The description of these expeditions will serve to show what may be done by small groups of keen mountaineers in grappling with all but the very highest peaks of the Himalaya. They show that with our greater knowledge and improved technique, and with the aid of increasingly efficient Himalayan porters, peaks of even the 25,000-feet standard may be successfully tackled by small, well-led parties.

Photograph by Dr. Visser.

A CARAVAN ON THE CHHUSKHU GLACIER.

Chapter VIII

HIMALAYAN PEOPLES

AMONG the most valuable results of the successive Everest expeditions has been the building up of a stern mountain tradition among the Sherpas and Bhutias of the Everest region. Both of these are of original Tibetan stock. They were mountain folk who had lived all their lives within sight or reach of the great peaks. From boyhood they had been accustomed to carrying loads on the mountain-sides and over high passes. They had the physique to climb the highest peaks. But they had not the technical training in the craftsmanship of mountaineering. Nor had they the vision.

Since the advent of the Everest expeditions a striking change has come over them. They have become much more than mere bearers of loads: they have developed into real mountaineers. Always possessed to some degree of the spirit of adventure, that spirit has now developed to such an extent that they eagerly rush to join any Himalayan expedition which comes out from Europe. In their acute though unconscious way they have tested the Englishmen on Everest, and come to the conclusion that they are men to be trusted and worth following. The climbers have led the way to where they also would like to go. In them, too, has arisen the ambition to climb Everest. Seeing the Englishmen facing danger has fortified *their* spirit. Pitting themselves against the mountain has been a splendid tonic for them. It has braced them up—set their blood tingling. They are bigger men for it. And if they have admired the climbers, no less have the climbers admired them—admired their staunch fidelity, their patient endurance, and their wonderful cheeriness. So climbers and porters have become firm comrades. And if the porters may have observed certain flaws in the climbers—occasional irascibility, for example—and the climbers have realized that the porters are not yet perfect saints but still retain a capacity for peccadilloes, both recognize that these are, after all, of small account in the big reckoning-up. In the face of great deeds on a great mountain they vanish like the morning mist before the sun ; and in the main the comradeship of climbers and porters stands out as something truly remarkable to have resulted from expeditions every one of which had failed to reach its goal.

For this result, no thanks that we should offer to the great founders of this new mountain tradition, Bruce and Norton and Somervell, can be too warm. To Bruce, companionship with these mountain people is as natural as the affection of two schoolboys for each other, though in many respects they may be quite unlike. He has lived, and fought, and worked, and climbed with them for years and years. He knows their traditions and upbringing. He knows their failings. He knows the point at which they will suddenly crumple up on a mountain, or go wrong in a town. But he knows their capacities for good. And to him, above all, we owe it that they have come on so strikingly since the Everest expeditions, and are so worthy of the esteem and affection in which they are now held.

Norton has not such a long and intimate association with them as Bruce has enjoyed, but he has had even better opportunities of facing mountain dangers in their company. And by the rescue which he organized with Mallory and Somervell of the marooned porters on the North Col he established the all-important principle that even at the risk of losing the chance to reach the summit the porters' lives must be saved. The summit must wait: porters' lives must come first.

Thirdly, comes Somervell with his bigness and breadth, his cheerfulness and warm humanity. He must have penetrated far into the heart of these responsive porters and helped in the fresh early days to establish the good tradition of mountain comradeship between climbers and porters.

What these first expeditions started Ruttledge carried on. He was well acquainted with the type. He had himself climbed with Sherpas in the mountain district which he had ruled for five years. He had found them "fine, free movers on a hillside, with the bold, open manners of the true hill man." And when, nine years after the previous expedition, he himself came to organize another expedition, he found these Sherpas and Bhutias pouring into Darjiling to enlist. Those selected were proud to be members of the expedition and eager to prove themselves true mountaineers. And it was not for the money that they came. They could make as much elsewhere. They came to make a name for themselves, and for the joy of the great adventure. To climb on Everest is, in the Sherpa cosmos, says Ruttledge, " the true riband of achievement."

Amongst those who came the outstanding figure was Lhakpa Chedi, who had been one of the " tigers " in the 1924 expedition. The question had arisen whether porters *could* carry a camp from 25,000 feet to the 27,000-feet level. Before these Everest expeditions were launched the highest point man had reached on a mountain was 24,600 feet. But that height had been reached by men without loads. Now men with loads were to be asked to climb to 27,000 feet. Would they do it? A party of porters before had refused to go farther; and it was highly probable that the four upon whom Norton had to rely would also refuse. But after hours of argument in the freezing early morning, Norton had at last persuaded three out of the four to carry a tiny tent and some provisions higher up the mountain, and Lhakpa Chedi had been one of the three. Norton had appealed to their imagination. He had painted a picture of the glory which would be theirs if they succeeded. He had told them how their names would be inscribed in letters of gold in the book which would be written to describe the exploit. The result had been that the little tent had been carried to a narrow cleft in the rocks at an altitude of 26,800 feet—some 11,000 feet higher than the top of Mont Blanc. It was a most gallant feat, and its great value lay in the establishment of a record. The thing had been done once, and therefore could be done again. Perhaps a point even higher could be reached. Man had found once that he could go higher than he had expected. He might find it so again.

And now Lhakpa Chedi, one of the three heroes who performed that feat, was eager to join another expedition. Since his great exploit he had been a very efficient head waiter in a Darjiling restaurant. He now proposed to join up as messman, and was joyfully accepted. But when the expedition reached Base Camp he could no longer be content with that humble rôle. He would be one of the porters on the mountain itself. And when he arrived on the mountain he would be one of the selected eight who would carry the camp highest. He would lead the others even higher than he had reached nine years before. But times proved bad. While at Camp V., at about 25,500 feet, a terrific storm came on. Three nights of unceasing storm had reduced the porters' strength, and food was running short. Instead of going higher, it became necessary to retreat lower, and even as it was, in the piercing cold Lhakpa Chedi lost two fingers. He was rendered incapable of further effort. He had not gained his ambition, but his presence among the porters had been of priceless value in heartening them for the enterprise.

Another instance of persistent courage was afforded by Ondi. He was one of the strongest of the Sherpa porters. In ordinary times at Darjiling he would have trouble with the police. But in times of stress upon the mountain he was a thruster. As the expedition was starting up the glacier to Everest he was stricken with double-pneumonia. On the very day he collapsed he had carried a load to Camp I. Recognizing that such a disease at such an altitude must almost certainly prove fatal, the British climbers despaired of his life. He was put to bed at once, given a continuous supply of oxygen, and watched all night by climbers and porters. Then it was decided to carry him down to lower altitudes in the Kharta Valley, five marches distant. It was a last hope, and his life was really despaired of. However, he reached Kharta safely. He recovered. And one month later, against medical orders, he returned to the Base Camp, carrying a heavy load on his back and demanding work on the mountain.

The porter hero of the 1933 expedition was perhaps the stout-hearted little Angtarke. He was one of those who had been with Lhakpa Chedi and forced to retreat. And he was the only one of that eight who was able to go high again. On 28th May a party set forth to re-establish Camp V. with twelve freshly-selected porters, of whom Angtarke was one. The next morning the attempt would be made to carry a camp to the 27,000-feet level. A biting wind was whistling across the

Photograph by Bentley Beetham.

PORTERS AT SEDONGCHEN.

ridge, and at about this same point Norton, nine years before, had had to spend hours in persuading the porters to go higher. This time, however, the fact that a tent had once been carried to nearly 27,000 feet had its psychological effect upon the porters. So when the climbers got up at 5 a.m. they found the eight porters ready and willing without any persuasion to make the needed effort. As a matter of fact, a start was not made till 8 a.m., because the cold was so severe that there was a great risk of frostbite, and also because the thermos flasks had not been capable of keeping the contents warm through the night. The porters were therefore sent back to their tents to make a fresh brew.

Then, carrying about ten pounds each, the porters followed the lead of Wyn Harris, Wager, and Longland. And on this critical day they showed themselves not just porters but real mountaineers. They had to pass over " the kind of ground where an accident is most likely to occur ; downward-sloping slabs offering no good ledges or holds." These slabs were evilly smooth and treacherous. Safety depended altogether on balance and the friction of the boot-nails. A rope would have been worse than useless, for if one man had slipped he would have carried the others with him. And in these exacting circumstances the porters showed an unexpected steadiness and ability. They were at home alike on the slabs and on the occasional patches of hard snow and frozen scree.

At the end of every fifty minutes a ten-minute halt was called. But the porters hardly needed it. Before the time was up most of them were pressing to get on again. The highest camp-level of the previous expedition was reached and passed. But at about 27,000 feet the angle of ascent suddenly steepened. And soon it became necessary to look for a camping site, for some of the men were at last beginning to show signs of exhaustion, and they would still have to be taken down to Camp IV. on the North Col before night set in. At last a small ledge was found. It was nowhere more than three feet wide, and it sloped outward. But *faute de mieux* it had to do. It was at an altitude of 27,400 feet, which was 600 feet higher than Norton's porters had reached in 1924, and 400 yards horizontally nearer the summit.

The men were quite ready to go higher still, but owing to the return to the North Col having yet to be made, that was not possible. As it was, that return turned out to be a highly dangerous operation, and was only successfully accomplished through the magnificent leadership of Longland, of which an account has been given at the close of Chapter II. Longland, bringing up the rear, persuaded the last and most tired of the men to persevere, till at last, just before dark, he himself as well as the porters, utterly exhausted, they reached Camp IVa. on the North Col. It was the biggest effort of the porters on any expedition, and only made possible by the men's hardihood and Longland's great leadership.

Next day, 30th May, they descended the North Col, and by then had recovered, for a diarist at Camp III., at the base of the North Col, records: "In the morning we were greatly cheered by the arrival of the 'tigers,' who yesterday established Camp VI. at 27,400 feet—a magnificent achievement, and easily the highest point to which loads have ever been carried. Most of them were looking as untouched as if they were hanging around Darjiling bazaar. Apparently Jack (Longland) took over shepherding the porters, although he was himself a very tired man. He put up a very wonderful show indeed."

But, lest we should get the notion that these porters are all supermen, and so miscalculate their possibilities on other expeditions, it is well to state that they have their deficiencies. This is not done in any way to disparage them—for English climbers also have their defects. It is only done to give due proportion to the picture.

As Ruttledge says, these Sherpas and Bhutias have limitations which are come upon very unexpectedly. At one time they will appear to be going strong and full of spirit. At the next they will suddenly give out. Here is an example. One of the porters who had carried the camp highest was Kipa Lama. On the way down he absolutely collapsed. At the North Col he was convinced that he was dead, and therefore could go no farther. He was treated by Dr. McLean, who found him physically very much alive. But his wits were scattered. He had lost control over himself. He had to be gently propelled from the rear down the dangerous ice of the North Col, while Wyn Harris and Wager steadied him with the rope down the steps. He conversed volubly on the dividing line between life and death. Then Brocklebank took him over, and came down with him on a short rope. " He slid most of the way on his bottom," says Brocklebank, " utterly wrecking the track, and with most of his weight on me in spite of my entreaties that he should stand up . . . if I'd slipped, Kipa and I would have gone for six all right. Also the poor old boy was affected in mind. He kept stopping and staring about him in a dazed sort of way. And where there was no fixed rope he seemed unable to see the track, and kept wandering all over the slopes." Eventually they reached Camp III. in safety. Afterwards he made a sufficiently complete recovery. And he was always very grateful to the climbers who had convinced him that he was still alive. But his case is a warning as to what may happen to even the best.

If the porters are not all supermen physically, neither are they all saints in the moral sphere. Some of them are, indeed, very human human beings. On the North Col, after a severe storm, one porter, though in the position of an under-Sirdar (a kind of non-commissioned officer), lost all sense of duty. He put a red sweet in his mouth, chewed it, and then spat on the snow to deceive Ruttledge into thinking that he was spitting blood. Two others were also very difficult to move—even though it was downward. One of them who, a few days before, had been the keenest of the

Photograph by Bentley Beetham.

A TIBETAN WOMAN.

keen and volunteering for the hardest jobs, now, with a slight frostbite, was a mere ragbag of self-pity. "It was the old story," reflects Ruttledge, "when the Sherpa once gets into the dumps he is a sorry inversion of his real self."

Besides these Sherpas and Bhutias, Ruttledge on the last expedition employed some pure Tibetans, and writes enthusiastically of them. Forty-six of them were brought from Sola Khombu in June. They came straight through from the Base Camp to Camp II. without a pause, superbly indifferent to altitude and the rough moraines, and content with any shelter for the night. With the wonderful aptitude of the Tibetans for building, they immediately set to work rolling the moraine boulders into position for a wall. Outer flies from tent were stretched overhead, and soon they had a fire going, tsampa was being cooked, and song and laughter were heard. They were quite ready to go to Camp III. or higher. They were, says Ruttledge, a grand lot, impervious to cold and fatigue, and apparently unaffected by any superstitious dread of the mountains.

This opens up a new vista. Might not Tibetans also, in addition to Sherpas and Bhutias, be included among the porters? They are born at, and pass their whole lives at, an altitude approximately the same as that of the summit of Mont Blanc. They must therefore be splendidly acclimatized to high altitudes. They are accustomed to the terrific winds of Tibet. And they are of a cheery, willing spirit. Clothed, booted, and equipped for climbing on Everest as have been the Sherpas and Bhutias, they might go as high as any.

Doubtless they, like the others, would show weaknesses and defects under the frightful strain of Everest. But while defects of these Himalayans must be reckoned with, they should not be made to fill too much of the picture. The main point is that there, ready to hand on both sides of the Himalaya, is a magnificent body of men with all the physical capacity to reach the summit—and men whose spirit has steadily responded to the higher and higher calls which have been made upon it. Now it is more a matter for the spirit than the body to decide the limit of what can be attained. The fact that men actually have carried loads to 27,40c feet, the further fact that those one or two who gave way under the strain afterwards perfectly recovered, and, lastly, the fact that these men by their deeds have won renown throughout the Himalaya and even in faraway Europe—all this will fortify and stabilize the spirit of porters in future expeditions. Gradually the texture of their spirit will become as firm as the texture of their bodies. And the utmost that these bodies are capable of doing, their spirit will drive them on to do.

Their reward should be that one of them should stand with an Englishman on the summit of that supreme peak, one side of which belongs to Tibet and the other to Nepal, but whose importance, as being the highest mountain in the world, was discovered by Englishmen.

The call of Everest has now been taken up by Himalayan people. The idea of climbing the mountain never occurred to these mountain races till it was put into their minds by islanders from the Atlantic Ocean. But now that it it is there, they rise to it as keenly as any European. The word has only to go round that there is to be another Everest expedition and scores swarm to Darjiling imploring to be taken on it. Given the lead, the response is sure.

But it is not only Sherpas and Bhutias who are so keen. Right along the Himalaya this spirit of adventure may be found. I first came across it on the journey to which I have already referred. Wali, the man who undertook to take me to India by the unknown Mustagh Pass over the main axis, was a Balti—a former inhabitant of Askoley, the village in Baltistan nearest to the Pass. He was of a different type from the Sherpas and Bhutias so well known on Everest expeditions. Those were of the Mongolian type. He was of a more "Aryan" type. Those were gay and cheery, and carefree. He was grave and sedate. He took very seriously the responsibility of conducting me across the Himalaya. He had promised that if I placed myself unreservedly in his hands he would land me on the Indian side of the Himalaya. And he felt the responsibility for keeping his promise.

No one could have more faithfully fulfilled his word than Wali did. He got together four other Baltis. They took charge of me as if I were an infant, and they did succeed in conveying me safely across the

Himalaya. But, looking back now, the interesting point to note is the relationship which sprang up between us. I felt an utter child in their hands, for I knew practically nothing about mountains, while they were all born and brought up in this very region. On the other hand, there were great risks to be run, and I felt responsibility for asking them to incur these for my sake. So, while I felt myself to be in their hands, I also felt them to be in mine. And I fancy they had the same kind of feeling in regard to me. There was a sense of mutual dependence between us.

And we saw each other very intimately during the six weeks we were together. For we forced a way together through the mountain by day. We fed together out of the same cooking-pot of an evening. And we slept alongside each other on the ground at night. Moreover, having nothing to distract us from the one enterprise upon which we were all engaged, our thoughts ran in common, too. Would Wali be able, after twenty-five years, to remember the way through the labyrinth of pathless mountains to the Mustagh Pass ? And when we got there should we be able to get over it, or would the accumulation of ice upon it make it utterly impracticable ? These were the questions which excited us all—including Wali himself.

As we accommodated ourselves to each other, I have no doubt their opinion of my mountaineering capacity remained pretty poor, but I was gratified to find that their faith in my *iqbal*—my good fortune—increased. This is important to establish with Himalayan people.

It cannot be deliberately achieved. It must grow of itself. But it is a most valuable thing when it does so spring up. It means that they have learned to have confidence in you. So when my Baltis had acquired faith in my *iqbal*, they would of themselves ask me to find a way over or round some obstacle which they had not themselves been able to surmount.

Who actually led over the Pass itself I cannot even now say for certain. I most certainly would not have ventured without Wali. I am equally certain that Wali would not have ventured without me. We reinforced each other. And I believe this will always be the case on Himalayan expeditions. Europeans and Himalayans will always have to depend upon each other and be at times the " child " and at times the leader to one another.

For some years the Baltis had the reputation of being poor mountaineers, and rather than employ them on the mountain the Duke of Abruzzi brought out Italian porters as well as guides. This was largely due to the bad name given to them by Mrs. Bullock-Workman. They certainly had not her tireless energy; and without sufficient food or proper equipment, or adequate spiritual inducement, they were not likely to show themselves at their best. But the Duke of Abruzzi, a perfect leader of men, detected their good qualities and afterwards saw that there had been no necessity for bringing men from Italy : the Baltis on the spot, properly cared for and equipped, were both fitted and willing to climb.

They are also good companions in the mountains. Ordinarily, they have a rather depressed, long-suffering, patient look about them, for they have a hard time of it keeping body and soul together in their remote mountain valleys. But gathered round the camp-fire at night, with their bodies well fed, good pay assured, and their minds free, they will tell long stories, sing, and even dance.

The next Himalayan people with whom I was brought in contact were the Gurkhas. In 1889 I had six with me on an exploration at the back of the Himalaya and into Hunza. They were from General Bruce's regiment, the 5th Gurkhas, and formed an escort for me as a protection against the Hunza raiders. Very different were they from the docile Baltis. The Gurkhas were bursting with good cheer, in almost perpetual laughter, except when a supernatural sternness came over them on parade. They were full of pride too—pride of their regiment and pride of themselves. I should not say that they had much initiative in the way of adventure, but they are ready enough to go on the riskiest adventure on the call of a leader they trust. General Bruce could take them anywhere. If they have a fault it is taking things too easy. I have been nearly killed through a Gurkha sentry sleeping at his post. Also they are prone to suffer from thirst when potent liquor is within sight. They have these two failings. But when strung up to be their best, that best is very good indeed. And a stout, sturdy, cheery Gurkha is as fine a comrade among the mountains as a man could wish for.

But of all the Himalayan peoples, those for whom I, personally, have the greatest regard are the men of Hunza. I first knew of them as the terror of the Central Asian plains and of the trade route between India and Turkestan. For two of the Baltis who took me over the Mustagh Pass had been captured by them and sold as slaves, and they told me lurid tales about them. But in 1889 I saw them in the very stronghold from which they issued on their raids—about the most secluded part of the whole Himalaya, and one which has never since been visited by a European. They were a wild, hardy-looking lot, but not savage or cruel. And finding that I was coming to see their Chief in order to stop the raids they at once became friendly, for they detested the raids as they suffered great hardships in making them, and got little of the booty—the Chief himself taking most. This first acquaintance was renewed when, two years later, I came to live amongst them. And I still keep up correspondence with the Chief, whom I assisted to instal in 1891.

In degree of cheerfulness they lie between the somewhat sad Baltis and the smiling Gurkhas. They have a certain gravity about them and solidity of character. Physically they are immensely hard, and it is said that their diet of barley, buckwheat, milk, occasional mutton, and dried apricots is ideal. On the shortest notice they are capable of making enormous effort. I have known one hundred of them, carrying rifles, ammunition, and food, march sixty-one miles in thirty-six hours, across the roughest mountain tracks. And this at only two hours' notice.

I myself am no mountaineer. But on one occasion I wanted to get across from the Hunza valley into the next valley westward, just to see from a military point of view whether the one valley was accessible from the other. It was a nice holiday expedition, with enough object in it to make it worth while. There was, of course, no track ; and there was no record or remembrance of any one having been that way before. We took no tent, and just made our way up the most likely-looking valley and trusted to luck to finding a way down the other side. Our luck held, and we did cross from the Hunza valley into the Ashkuman valley, thus securing our object. But what I enjoyed most was the opportunity of seeing these Hunza men at work. They were on their mettle, and went at it with that tremendous earnestness of purpose which, like children, they would throw into whatever they did. Then, of an evening, after the day's work was over and they would settle down to enjoy themselves by telling stories, I could see that they had lots of fun in them and could enjoy the light side of life as well as face the stern.

The Hunza people love dancing too, and making-up and performing plays. None of them could read or write in my days, but they could be very eloquent when they were stating a case on which they had their hearts set, and capable of both giving and receiving chaff. The play they made up caricaturing a British officer out shooting is well known. Also they were keen polo players. Altogether a most fascinating people I call them. And their home, in amongst peaks of 24,000 feet and 25,000 feet in height, and dominated by the exquisite Rakapushi Mountain, is one of the most glorious in the world. It was a rare privilege to have had the chance of seeing these people in their own country in their original state—"unspoilt state," as I suppose it will soon come to be called.

I have been describing what we think of Himalayan people. Just as interesting is what Himalayan people think of us. A few years ago an American traveller induced his Ladaki caravan leader, Rasul, to write out his experiences. This by, literally, the sweat of his brow, he did. He could just write, very slowly, a very "pidgin" English. But by beginning at seven o'clock in the morning, shutting himself up alone, and working all day, he did produce something for Mr. Barrett which Mr. Barrett was able to get published. And so well did Rasul tell his story, for, like most Himalayans he was a born story-teller, that the book went into a second edition. And in this book—*A Servant of Sahibs*—we can see most perfect pictures of how we appear to these hill-men.

I myself am fortunate enough to appear in a halo of glory, because Rasul happened to make his first journey with me when I was conducting a political mission to Central Asia. He was still a boy and bursting with enthusiasm to cross the mountains to the mysterious cities of Yarkand and Kashgar in Central Asia. He managed to get taken on as a help to one of the caravan men, and seeing me receiving and being received by high Chinese officials and lavishly dispensing costly presents—at Government expense—I naturally appeared as something a little short of a god in his unsophisticated eyes. And Barrett and Mrs. Barrett had god-like qualities of a more human description, as they always treated him with extreme kindness. But one Englishman had a very hot temper, and caused Rasul much pain—physical and mental. And a certain noble lord grievously disappointed him by presenting him with only an old coat at the end of hard and arduous journeyings.

Speaking generally, we may say that we appear to these childlike mountain peoples always in high lights. We are either gods or demons. Some ordinary act of kindness is magnified into a deed of superhuman generosity. Some hasty rebuke is intensified into a malignant design.

But Rasul does not make himself out any stained-glass window saint. He had been given some brandy by his master on a bad night after crossing a pass, and he had found it so delicious that he had concocted with another servant a plan for taking a little more when the master was not looking. They agreed that it was wrong, but they would overcome that difficulty by drinking it first and repenting afterwards. When they got back to Leh they would go to a mulla, tell him of their misdeed, and then repent. But when he was at last back in Leh he found himself in trouble over somebody else's wife and sent to jail. On the whole, though, he seems to have enjoyed life in jail and found it a haven of rest after his hard travels. His relations would bring him plenty to eat, he would have no work, and he would spend the nights in the thrilling pastime of swopping stories with kindred spirits.

And in Rasul again we see that same love of adventure so common among Himalayan people. Of his own initiative he made out this life for himself. He was determined to go off with some caravan across the mountains. My passing through Leh gave him the opportunity. He seized it, and eventually rose to be a recognized leader of caravans. Before he died he was appointed the Government Agent for regulating the caravan traffic between India and Turkestan. In spite of those little incidents of the brandy and another man's wife, he was highly respected by the caravan community and by European leaders of expeditions.

One general characteristic of all these Himalayan people has to be noticed. They are by nature religious. Some are Muslims, some Hindus, some Buddhists, but every one of them is in his own simple way religious. He is conscious of some Power, mightier far than himself, at work in the world about him. He has very primitive and vague ideas as to the mode of operation of this Power, and as to the way in which he is related to It. But he regards It as in some fashion a Personal

Power who expects him to be good. He must be careful to avoid incurring the anger of this tremendous Power, and he must ingratiate himself with Him so that he may deserve, or anyhow receive, His blessing. The best means of approach to this Power is through a Hindu priest or Buddhist lama, or a Muslim mulla. These know more about the ways of God and how His anger may be appeased and His blessing secured. But if these are not available, the hill-men will themselves invoke the blessing of God before they enter upon some dangerous enterprise, and often I have seen them throw out their arms in a great gesture of thanksgiving when they have come safely through the danger.

Above all else, the European must avoid the faintest curl of derision at such evidence of religious feeling. Rather should he encourage every sign and symptom, for there is a deep element of truth in these exhibitions, and the expression of their religious feelings gives strength of purpose and stability of character. Superstition there may be in some of their ideas, but the main conviction—that they are in the hands of a Power mightier than themselves which expects them to shun the evil and do the good, and will punish their evil deeds and reward their good—they are perfectly justified in holding. They *are* in the hands of such a Power—and so is the European mountaineer himself. And the more the Himalayan hill-men and the European mountaineer realize their common kinship as creatures of that Power, as alike animated by It and dependent on it, the more likely are they to be successful in their common endeavour.

Bruce, Norton, and Ruttledge were very wise in encouraging the Everest porters to seek the blessing of the lama in the monastery at the foot of Everest. And it was sound instinct of these British leaders to go with their followers. The more we share our religion the better. We are all animated by the same Holy Spirit of God, and whatever tends to emphasize this intimate kinship of *spirit*—which is so much closer than the very distant *blood* relationship—is all to the good.

BOOK II: REFLECTION

CHAPTER IX

UNITY WITH NATURE

THAT the Himalaya is the most prominent feature on the face of the earth is well known. What is not so well recognized is the influence it is bound to exert upon the human race. Already it has had a profound effect upon the people of India. For thousands of years the most spiritual among them have been inspired by the Himalaya. To this day multitudes of them every year make pilgrimage to sacred shrines at the sources of the great rivers which arise there. And now the influence of the Himalaya is extending to Europeans, and, through them, to the whole world.

But upon neither Indians nor Europeans has the Himalaya yet exercised anything like so profound an influence as it is bound to exert in the future. For the Indians are no real lovers of mountains. They have hitherto rather feared than loved them. They have never dared to face them straightly and strive to climb their highest summits. And as for Europeans, our love of mountains is only in its initial stages. With the Himalaya in particular we are only beginning to be acquainted. What we Europeans shall be wanting to know then, as we accept the challenge of Everest, and come to closer grips with the highest summits, is what effect the Himalaya will ultimately have upon the human race. Already we have realized the astounding altitudes of the supreme peaks, and have luxuriated in the richness and variety of the vegetation which clothes their lower slopes. But as we become more familiar with the Himalaya a question which will be perpetually arising is: What will be the eventual effect upon us of this deeper intimacy with the most impressive object in Nature? The contemplation of any great mountain has an elevating influence upon a man. To what heights will the Himalaya raise men as they pit themselves against its loftiest peaks and brace themselves to face its utmost rigours? This is what we would be told.

Indians already see the vision, though as yet only dimly and not in the full splendour in which they will eventually behold it as they come to love the mountains more. And there are a few of us Europeans who have spent many years of our lives in the Himalaya, who have seen something of what these mountains mean to the more spiritual Indians, and who have caught some of that meaning ourselves. General Bruce is such a one. He has climbed in the Himalaya more than any living person, and the more he has seen of these wonderful mountains the more passionately he has come to love them. Hugh Ruttledge, the leader of the 1933 Everest Expedition, who had served as Deputy-Commissioner in the Himalayan District of Almora, is another. I may count myself a third. For I was born in the Himalaya, have lived for years there, have eleven times crossed the entire breadth of the range from the plains of India to the plains of Turkestan or Tibet and back, and have seen all the very highest peaks. And there are others like Bruce, Ruttledge and myself who have spent many years in the Himalaya, or have gone there on leave for big-game shooting year after year, and have become increasingly devoted to the Himalaya as they have come to know it better.

Then railways, motor cars, and aeroplanes are making the Himalaya yearly more accessible to those Europeans whose lives are spent in India in the Government, Civil or Military, Service, or for purposes of business. These improved means of conveyance are also bringing from Europe itself, and from America, more persons who come out with the specific object of travelling in the Himalaya or climbing some great peak. Expeditions great and small penetrate deeper in among the mountains, and climb higher and higher peaks. And these mountaineers write books about what they have seen and achieved, and thus attract much attention to the Himalaya.

In consequence of all this activity the glories of the Himalaya are becoming known throughout the world. The appetite to see them is being whetted. The exploits of the climbers in the Himalaya thrill the souls of mountaineers in every country, and even those who can never hope to see the splendour of a Himalayan peak catch from the description something of the glow which the climbers themselves had felt.

And there is just now beginning a contact which may have important results in the future. Climbers of the highest peaks have to employ as porters some of the hardier peoples of the Himalaya, and between European climbers and Himalayan porters a strong feeling of comradeship is growing up. This is important enough. But not nearly so important in its eventual results as the touch which is just beginning to be made between the European lover of the mountains and those sensitively spiritual Hindus from the plains of India who come to visit the sacred shrines of the Himalaya, and who, having come there, are as impressed as their far remote predecessors had been by the solemn grandeur of the mountains and by the exquisite beauty of the Himalayan scenes. There is a deep affinity between the European mountain-lover and the Indian pilgrim to the Himalaya which closer contact between the two will most beneficially strengthen. The more vigorous European will stimulate the more passive Indians, and give strength and substance, and perhaps clarity also, to their thoughts and feelings about the Himalaya, while the Indians, with their more sensitive refinement of feeling, will communicate a greater delicacy to the robuster European.

Cynics like Dean Inge may say that the hills of England are good enough for them. And there is some truth in this. We all know what an influence

MAKALU AT DAWN.

the hills of Cumberland and Westmorland had upon Wordsworth. But that is not the point. Beautiful as is the influence which the hills of England exert upon Englishmen, the impression which the first sight of a supreme Himalayan peak makes upon a man is of an altogether different order. The sight of even the highest hill in England does not set him gasping as does the sight of a Himalayan peak—and gasping with something more than mere delight. Nor is he impressed for a lifetime by an English hill as he is by a Himalayan giant. An English rose makes one kind of impression upon us, and an English hill quite another. The one does not rule out the other ; it supplements it. But no one who ever had the chance of going to the Himalaya should miss it. For he will find there something different from what he can get anywhere else in the world—something both more expanding and more elevating. He will be a bigger man for the experience.

He will be more likely to gain such inspiration if he can go to the mountains with ample leisure for enjoyment of their beauty—if he can go there in some sense as a pilgrim and make for himself the opportunity of getting away for a time from the fret and worry and stress of life, so as to give his mind a chance of "settling" and of seeing things in their due proportion. In such case there may come to him special moments when he will be in a peculiarly receptive mood, and able to take in to the full the wonderful impressions the Himalaya has to give. The like of these moments, if they come, he may never know elsewhere. In them he may have the experience of a lifetime. During those precious times of calm and receptivity all his previous learning and all his previous knowledge of life may be summed up in a single experience. It may be a case not only of his mind but of his whole personality, feeling as well as intelligence, responding to the mighty impression being made upon it. And he may then get an insight into the deepest nature of things such as he may never acquire without this quiet for reflection, and without that incitement to the soul which these greatest of all mountains give.

This will be more possible if he has previously steeped his mind, firstly, in what science has to tell about the immensity of the scale on which the Himalaya is built, and, secondly, in the experiences of those ardent mountaineers who have set forth to climb the highest peaks. The adventures of the climbers who boldly assailed the highest peaks, and more especially those who attempted to scale Everest itself, have already been described. The tale of science may now be briefly told.

The Himalayan system proper—that is, exclusive of the Hindu Kush extension—is over fifteen hundred miles in length. That is to say, if placed in Europe it would extend from Mont Blanc to the Caucasus. That will give an idea of the length of the Himalaya. As to the height of its highest peaks, these are :

1 peak	over	29,000	feet in height
3 peaks	„	28,000	„ „ „
6 „	„	27,000	„ „ „
18 „	„	26,000	„ „ „
49 „	„	25,000	„ „ „
86 „	„	24,000	„ „ „

Thus there are at least eighty-six peaks in the Himalaya higher than any other mountains in the world. In a general way the peaks in the Himalaya are about twice the height of the peaks in the Alps. The Himalaya is incomparably the most prominent feature on the face of the earth.

How this stupendous range of mountains came into being has been studied by geologists. And the startling outcome of investigations is that it was once at the bottom of the sea. Until a comparatively recent date in the geological time-scale, says Sir Henry Hayden, the geologist,* all the northern part of what is now the Himalaya was covered by a great sea in which the deposition of sediment had occurred for a vast period. But, in the middle of the Tertiary period—that is, according to the scale in the new Geological Museum, about fifty million years ago—a period of crust-movement set in and the floor of the sea began to rise and to be thrown into a series of long, parallel, wave-like folds. This was the first faint origin of what is now the Himalaya. What was the origin of the forces

* *The Geography and Geology of the Himalaya Mountains*, by Burrard and Hayden.

which brought about this upheaval can at present only be conjectured. It may have been caused by a horizontal thrust from the north. The sediments of the sea may have been forced against the northern coast of the once continuous Indo-African continental mass which stood like a buttress in the path of the advancing earth-waves.

But what caused the thrust? Geologists think it may have been caused by a contraction of the earth owing to loss of heat. If there were such contraction the rate of contraction of the inner nucleus would be greater than that of the crust. The crust, through contracting more slowly, would be left unsupported, and in adapting itself to the new core, would become wrinkled. This appears to geologists to be the most likely cause of those first faint upheavals which, continuing through hundreds, thousands, and millions of years, eventually resulted in the Himalaya Mountains.

Then, as the crests of the earth-waves rose above the waters of the seas, they would be exposed to erosion by rain and weather. They would be like the islands of the Malay Archipelago to-day. These islands are, indeed, in process of elevation, and one or other may be the Mount Everest of a million years hence. The rising crest of the earth-waves as they rose from the sea and were eroded would become broken and irregular, and a river system would gradually be developed. But while this erosive process was continually tending to wash away the incipient mountains, the elevating forces would also be in action and would be raising the mountain faster than it was being denuded. Gradually, in the latter part of the Eocene period—about thirty million years ago—the mountain system of the Himalaya would have developed.

In addition to this general upheaval there were, however, other forces at work. Geologists have noticed that, of the great peaks, almost all of those of 25,000 feet or more in height are composed of granite, gneiss, and associated crystalline rocks. These higher peaks are assumed to be due to special elevatory forces. The earth is believed to consist of concentric shells of different composition round a central nucleus of very heavy material, probably nickel iron. It is very hot within, and the outer shell or crust is of granite, about 200,000 feet in thickness, floating on a substratum of basalt. During the development of the Himalaya as a mountain range it is supposed that vast masses of this granite welled up from below, forcing their way through and lifting up the pre-existing sedimentary rocks above. Owing to dissimilarity of composition and structural weakness in certain portions of the earth's crust, movement would be more intense at some points than at others. In consequence, the granites would be locally raised into more or less dome-like masses standing above the general level of the growing range. Then these masses would be subsequently carved by the process of erosion into clusters of peaks—for it is noticeable that the great peaks of the Himalaya do occur in clusters : such as the Kangchenjunga cluster, the Everest cluster, and the K_2 cluster.

This is the conjectured history of the Himalaya. But that we may the better understand the stupendous scale on which the world is built, we will examine the Himalaya from another point of view. We have seen that it is by far the greatest range of mountains on the earth. We are impressed enough by the sight of Mont Blanc. But Everest is nearly twice its altitude. Now we have to realize that, staggering as is the height of the Himalayan giants, they are, in comparison with the earth as a whole, scarcely perceptible excrescences. If they were represented strictly to scale on an ordinary library globe, and any one were to pass his finger over the surface of the globe, he would not be able to detect their existence. Everest itself would only be a roughness one-thirtieth of an inch in height on a globe forty inches in diameter—and that is a very large globe. On an ordinary globe the Himalaya would be represented by a slight protuberance about as high as the thickness of the edge of the page upon which this is printed.

This will give us some conception of the size of the planet on which this mighty Himalaya forms a hardly noticeable protuberance. Yet the earth is only a tiny droplet from the sun. And the sun, as we can see from those wonderful photographs of the starry heavens which are now available, is only one amongst millions of other stars.

And when we come to the age of the Himalaya we have another indication of the immensity of things. The Himalaya Mountains are spoken of by geologists as of recent origin. But, by recent, they mean that they are at least thirty million years old. They are only young in comparison with other ranges, the age of which may be in the order of five hundred million years, and with the age of the earth, which may be about two thousand million years. While the sun itself may be two or three million million years old.

Whether, therefore, we consider the size and height or the age of the Himalaya, and bring them into comparison with the universe as a whole, we realize that the scale of things is immense beyond all power of comprehension.

But naturalists also, as well as geologists, should be consulted if the would-be pilgrim to the Himalaya is to gather an impression not only of the immensity of things, but also of the abundance and variety of life. For these mountains can give an impression both of the vastness of the scale on which the world is built, and also of the marvellous variety of living things which this planet can produce. To reach the great peaks we have to pass through the vast forests which clothe the lower ridges and valley bottoms. In the Eastern Himalaya these valley bottoms are only a few hundred feet above the sea-level, almost in the tropics, and subjected to very heavy rainfall. Consequently, the vegetation and insect life there is of tropical luxuriance and variety. In the Western and more Northerly Himalaya the climate is more temperate, and the rainfall not so excessive; the vegetation is therefore not so super-abundant. Yet there also life is abundant, and the traveller cannot fail to be impressed by its variety and beauty.

The traveller may reflect, also, that these self-same forests of the Eastern Himalaya have existed where they now are, not for mere centuries or thousands of years, but for millions. For twenty or thirty millions of years trees and plants have grown there in one great forest life ; and again we are reminded of the tremendous scale on which the Himalayan world is built.

In these tropical and semi-tropical forests—and I speak more especially now of the Sikkim forest on the way to Kangchenjunga, Tibet, and Everest—there is not the great silence of the higher regions, for there is always the purr of innumerable insect life. But there is a curious hush, and a feeling that intense and vivid life is vibrating all about us. And there is indeed a superabundant profusion of life of the greatest variety—great, straight-stalked trees rising in some cases to two hundred feet in height, and hydrangea-like shrubs ; climbers as thick as cables, and the most delicate ferns ; and all mixed together without the monotony so characteristic of the planted forests of Europe.

In the lowest and hottest parts of the Teesta Valley, up which lies the route to Everest, are tropical oaks nearly fifty feet in girth, stately sal trees, screw-pines, palms of many kinds, tree-ferns forty feet in height, bamboos, and plantains. Enormous climbers almost strangle the trees, and innumerable vines and peppers festoon themselves from tree to tree and branch to branch. Most delicate ferns and mosses there are too—

TREE-FERNS IN SIKKIM.

four kinds of light and graceful maidenhairs, the *Osmunda regalis*, and a gigantic fern with fronds five yards in length. Climbing ferns also clothe the trunks and branches of the trees, all giving an impression of elegance and grace.

Most noticeable, though, in these lower tropical forests are the orchids. We cannot say that they are so beautiful as the orchids of Brazilian forests, but perhaps only there are they surpassed. Four hundred and fifty species are to be found in the Sikkim forests, of which the most common are the dendrobiums and cymbidiums, well known in cultivation here in Europe. Marvellously beautiful are they as they are seen suspended from the branches of the trees amidst the ferns and creepers. Gems of immaculate perfection—purple, golden yellow, pale yellow, pink, white, and violet in colour, and all of that exquisite waxy texture which gives such a sense of finish and endurance.

At the level of Darjiling the most tropical plants and trees disappear, and magnolias, rhododendrons, alder, walnut, and hornbeams appear. The rhododendrons are the special glory of the forest at this altitude. The scarlet *r. arboreum*, so common all along the Himalaya as far north as Simla and the Kangra Valley, gives a glowing splash of colour. The splendid *r. grande*, or *argenteum*, which grows to a height of thirty to forty feet and bears waxy flowers of a yellowish-white suffused with pink, is another noticeable object. Altogether there are thirty species. There are still palms and plantains and bamboos, and amongst flowers, balsams, strawberries, gloxinias, speedwells and forget-me-nots, violets, primulas, anemones, delphiniums, and saxifrages. And in the Sikkim Valley may be found the glorious *lilium giganteum*, standing ten feet high, with fourteen flowers of the purest white growing on a single stalk.

Higher still in Sikkim are larch, birch, juniper, cherry, and, besides a rich abundance of primulas of the most varied kinds, purple, yellow, pink, and white, we find gentians of the deepest blue, golden potentillas, delicate anemones, fritillaries, balsams, ranunculas, lovely light-blue poppies, a great rose with single blossoms as large as the palm of one's hand.

When we reach the 13,000-feet level, the forest thins out, and low-growing birch, silver fir, mountain ash, berberis, and many stunted rhododendrons and azaleas predominate, while there are still gentians, geraniums, potentillas, campanulas, delphiniums, anemones, primulas, and some ferns.

As we near the snow-line the forest entirely disappears, and there only remain the most stunted rhododendrons and tiny primulas, saxifrages, and gentians.

Just as varied, abundant, and interesting as the flower and tree life is the insect life. And of the insects the butterflies are the most noteworthy. They are to the insect world what the orchids are to the plant world. Though here again the forests of Brazil seem to produce even more gorgeous butterflies than Sikkim can show, for none in the Himalaya can compare in colour with the radiant *morpho cipris*. More than six hundred species of butterflies there are in Sikkim, some of the most daring colours, others dim and shy, and only too anxious to avoid detection. There are two species of the most splendid bird-butterflies, measuring from six to eight inches across the wing, green on the upper side, and tipped with yellow. Forty-two species of swallow-tails there are, and no less than one hundred and fifty-four of " blues," and the curious leaf-butterfly which, when flying, discloses a most beautiful deep violet-blue, but when settled exactly resembles a leaf—even to the veins. Moths are even more numerous and varied than the butterflies. There are about two thousand species. One of them, the Atlas moth, measures nearly a foot across the wings.

Other insects are the pestilential mosquitoes, the noisy crickets and cicadæ, endless varieties of beetles, curious praying-insects and walking-stick insects, flies, lantern flies, and, of course, innumerable ants, bees, wasps, and flies.

Bird life is not abundant : it is indeed surprisingly scarce. But it is varied. There are between five and six hundred species. On the one hand are the great lammergeyer vultures known all along the Himalaya, and on the other there are the tiny flower-peckers. Here again, as with the orchids and the butterflies, the Himalaya cannot claim to have the most brilliant representatives in the world. It has no birds-of-paradise, and no humming-birds. But it does have glittering little sun-birds, and many species of fly-catchers, including the beautiful paradise fly-catcher.

Then there is the handsome monaul pheasant and the blood-pheasant ; the delightful, friendly little bulbuls, the fairy blue-bird of glistening cobalt blue upon velvet black, the European and other cuckoos, and kingfishers. Of birds of prey there are eagles of eleven species, peregrine falcons, owls, and kites. Of game birds, besides pheasants, there are quails, partridges, jungle-fowl, woodcock. Also there are pigeons, doves, jays, magpies, bulfinches, rose-finches, larks, tits, wagtails, parrots, twelve species of thrush and ten of robins, and many kinds of water birds—ducks, crane, storks, heron, cormorants.

Reptiles also are fully represented in the animal life. The largest is the python. Others are the cobra, four species of vipers, handsome whip snakes. Then there are lizards, frogs and toads, many of them very prettily coloured. And the most obtrusive of all on our notice are the horrible leeches—tiny, but countless in number.

Rising in the animal scale there are some eighty species of mammals, including three of monkeys, eight of cats, two of dogs, two of mongooses, two of bears, five of polecats and weasels, three of otters, four of squirrels, eight of rats and mice, four of deer, three of goats, and one of sheep. Tigers only occasionally come up into the forest from the plains, but the leopard is common. And elephants, in order to escape from the flies in the plains, have made a wonderful track up into the mountains.

This is a long, and perhaps wearisome, catalogue, derived from information collected by naturalists ;

and even this is not complete. But the mere enumeration is enough to impress us with the extraordinary variety of life in the Eastern Himalaya.

Finally we come to man. Neither in Sikkim nor anywhere else along the Himalaya are there any absolutely primitive men, like the Kols of Central India or the Todas of Southern India. But there live in Sikkim a people who are essentially a forest people, and are in perfect harmony with forest life. These are the Lepchas, a delightful, docile, amiable people with a wonderful knowledge of forest lore, as acute of sight and sound as the animals themselves, and almost as light and agile; knowing also the properties for good or ill of the forest produce—the roots, fruits, berries, leaves, and bark of plants and trees—and most deft and skilful in the use of bamboos, leaves, and grasses. They live in bamboo houses, and nowadays wear clothes. But fortunately they remain a real forest people, and by observing them in their lives we are able to surmise how it was that man rose into pre-eminence among the animals.

So much as regards the forests of the Eastern Himalaya. The forests of the Western Himalaya present a less abundant and a less varied life. But they are more pleasant for the traveller because they are drier and cooler, and less afflicted with tormenting insects. And being thinner, more glimpses of the snows beyond may be obtained. Moreover, if the plant and tree life be not so overwhelmingly prolific, it yet possesses a wonderful beauty of its own. Supreme is the stately deodar, so well known to visitors to Simla and other hill stations, and Kashmir, and known also here in the gardens of England as a single-stemmed, drooping-branched cousin of the cedar of Lebanon. And forests in which this graceful tree predominates have a special fragrance which lingers long in the memory of those who know it. Except in Kashmir, there are also the brilliant scarlet rhododendrons, so conspicuous among the deeper foliage in springtime. Then there is the long-leafed pine, commonly known as the chir, a red, rough-barked tree which will find a footing in the barest, craggiest rock slopes ; and many trees familiar in Europe, such as chestnuts, walnuts, sycamores, birches, and poplars.

The hillsides in the Western Himalaya are also more cultivated than in the Eastern, and there is a larger and more varied population. None are so primitive and so distinctly a forest people as the Lepchas. We are among real tillers of the soil. But they are sturdy people, capable of enduring great hardships in the higher mountains, and all of them most likeable. My own personal chief liking is for the men of Hunza, who live in a deep valley presided over by that most beautiful peak, Rakapushi, over 25,000 feet in height. These Hunza men were formerly raiders into Central Asia. But these raids were conducted under orders from their chief, and signified no predatory instinct on the part of the raiders. They only betokened that the Hunza men were hardy and enterprising. The Sherpa and Bhutias have made for themselves a great name as porters on Everest expeditions. But the men of Hunza, when they in turn come to be employed as porters on great Himalayan expeditions, will prove themselves just as worthy mountaineers.

Then in the lower ranges of the Western Himalaya are to be found knightly families of Rajputs of very ancient lineage, ruling over small hill estates—very brave in old times, and very courtly still. And in Kashmir live the Kashmiri Pandits, the most intellectual of all the Himalayan people, and in sheer mental capacity equal to any in the world.

In summing up what we see in the Himalaya below the snow-line, what most obviously strikes us is the profusion—the overabounding and seemingly wasteful profusion—of life, and with this prolific life the multitudinous varieties of forms. Indeed, countless as are the individual plants, trees, insects, animals, birds, and men, no two, even of the same species, are precisely alike in size, form, and colour. Each differs from all others in some slight respect.

The abundance and variety of life is evident enough. But as we look closer into the life of the forest other important characteristics emerge.

One is the extraordinary intensity of life. In the forest we experience an almost overpowering stillness. The rush and whirr and clang of life in a city are forgotten. Hardly a breath of air stirs the leaves. A great stillness broods over all. Yet, as we think of it, there must be a deep intensity of living all around. Take one of these tree monarchs, for example. How else than by deep intensity did it build itself up, delicately selecting and surely absorbing into itself the elements it needed from the soil, from the water, from the air, and from the sunshine? How else did it raise itself, dead against the force of gravity, two hundred feet into the air? How else did it maintain itself thus for hundreds of years? And, most remarkable of all, how else did it, year after year, produce flowers and thousands of seeds, each one of which was capable of reproducing its parent? Life of the intensest must be in each plant and tree. And if in them, how much more in the insects, animals, and birds?

It is, of course, this abundance and intensity of life which necessitates the well-known struggle for existence. So crowded is the forest life that there is a struggle among the trees and plants even for standing room. Then the food from the soil which plants need, though abundant, is limited, and necessarily there is a struggle for it among the plants, even when they have found standing room. Air may, for all practical purposes, be considered unlimited, but sunshine may be restricted by the closeness of the trees. The forest is in deep shade, and trees have to struggle upward to reach the light, while shrubs and plants have to do as best they may in the dimness of twilight. Then the plant world has to struggle with the animal world, for the animal world sustains itself not directly from the soil and sunshine, but indirectly through the plant world. Consequently, plants have to struggle against the animals, birds, and insects, and these latter have to struggle with one another for the limited supply of plant food. Further, certain animals and birds feed not directly on plants, but indirectly through eating other animals or birds. Beasts and birds of prey are engaged in a struggle for other animals or birds.

The result is a stern, selfish, and sometimes brutal struggle for existence, in which the fittest survive, and the weak, the old, and the unfit go to the wall.

Yet this is not the whole story. There is not only the keen but pitiless struggle between the individuals ; there is also in the forest life as a whole close interdependence and mutual aid. No one single individual is there by himself or itself alone. All are closely connected in one whole, and interdependent upon one another. Trees and plants by the bright colour or far-reaching fragrance of their flowers attract butterflies, moths, bees, and other insects to sip of their nectar. In return, the insect unconsciously serves the plant by conveying its pollen to fertilize another flower. The fertilized flower bears seeds, some of which are hidden in fruits and berries. And these furnish food for birds and animals. Plant and insect thus mutually benefit each other, and both benefit the birds and animals. In many such ways as these the individuals not only struggle with one another, but are dependent upon and benefit one another.

In this interdependence plants and animals adapt themselves to one another and to the general life of the forest. Adaptation to surroundings is as marked as the struggle. In the long process of years the plant learns to adapt itself to the insect, and the insect to the plant; the orchid to the bee and the bee to the orchid. In their search for food plants have developed sensitive tips to their roots, enabling them to feel for suitable constituents, and leaves also capable of gathering nourishment for the plant or tree from the air and sunshine they have developed. Similarly, animals have developed eyes and ears enabling them to search for food and avoid enemies.

But living things do not merely adapt themselves to their immediate surroundings: they strive to rise above them. Whether this is due to some hidden inner impulse alone, or to some stimulus from without, or to both, the result is that life in the forest is not on a dead level; it is graded. There is a scale of being. Some plants are higher in the scale for plants, and some animals in the scale for animals, than others. There is higher and lower. The orchid is higher than the moss, and the monkey than the mole.

And when we think of the surroundings to which plants and animals adapt themselves, we may reflect that those surroundings are not only the forest itself and the air and the sunshine, but the whole universe. And it may have been from the universe at large that came the stimulus which aroused in the individual plants or animals this striving, not merely to adapt themselves to their immediate surroundings, but to rise above them on to a higher level of being.

From this wider and nobler environment may also

have come not only the reaching upward but the reaching forward impulse. For deep in the foundations of life is the impulse to mate and propagate. Some urge within the individual responds to some stimulus without to carry itself forward. And many plants, as well as birds and animals, are so solicitous for the welfare of their offspring that they will sacrifice much for it. The struggle for existence gives way to readiness of the parent to sacrifice itself that its offspring may live. The countless instances of parental devotion are too well known for there to be any need to describe one.

In reviewing these leading characteristics of forest life we cannot help remarking the purposiveness which runs all through it. There is plenty of chance. By chance one berry drops into the river, is swept away to the ocean, and is wasted—for the time being. By chance another berry is eaten by a bird, the hard seed is excreted, falls upon good ground, and grows into a beautiful tree. Chance plays its part. But that marvel of ingenuity and beauty, the flower of an orchid, is not produced by chance. The odds are infinity to one against the millions of millions of the ultra-microscopic ultimate particles of matter having come together by chance to form the eye of an eagle. Everywhere we see adaptation, and everywhere we see selection. And where there is adaptation, and where there is selection, there is purposiveness—striving for some object. There is choosing, discrimination, rejection. This must be with some end in view which the choosing individual is striving to attain. Purpose governs the adaptations and selections.

But observation of life in the forest gives no indication that the end in view is anything closed and final, like the great ship *Queen Mary*. We do not see evidence of some thing being built up and slowly growing towards completion as the *Queen Mary* will be when she sets forth on her voyage. Rather do we observe a perpetual spring of creative activity like a painter turning out picture after picture, or a poet poem after poem. Forms of higher and higher perfection come welling forth from some inexhaustible source. The future is not closed in front. There is no end to what may be.

So when we dispassionately view the forest life as a whole, we would not describe it as " red in tooth and claw." Callousness, cruelty, pain, hunger, thirst, there are. The mother killed and the young dying from need of food, or cold or wet. The old and infirm dragging miserably to their end for want of any to care for them. Yet, consciously or unconsciously, the animals and plants aid one another as well as struggle against one another. And the final impression which the life in the forest leaves upon us is not one of misery and depression, but of joy. Life there is keyed up to its fittest. And because the birds and animals are fit, they enjoy themselves. There is joy in the struggle. And insensibly permeating the whole is this effort to press forward to a higher level of being. So there is an élan as well as joy. Life in the forest is hard, but it is happy.

Now man himself is coming forward through the Himalayan forest, first to adapt himself to the conditions of life at the highest altitude, and then to rise above them. Himalayan people and Tibetans had adapted themselves to altitudes equal to the summit of Mont Blanc. They had lived and grown wheat and barley at 15,000 feet. They had risen above their immediate surroundings by their life in monasteries at 16,000 feet. But the Himalayan peoples had never attempted to rise to the highest heights. This remained for Europeans to attempt, and for a century past men from Europe have been coming to the Himalaya to scale higher and higher heights, to adapt themselves to these loftier altitudes, and eventually not only to adapt themselves but to surpass them.

To enumerate all who have come out is unnecessary here. We have been concerned with the challenge which Everest has made to men to climb not only it but also the other great summits of the Himalaya, and come to such close quarters with the mountains that they may know and understand them.

And the attempt to reach the summit of the highest mountain in the world may be taken as symbolical of this striving in the heart of all living things to do something more than only adapt themselves to their surroundings: to stand superior to them. Man, as the crown of creation, in striving not merely to adapt himself to the loftiest regions, but to rise in spirit above them, is surpassing himself and reaching upward to a higher level of being.

Already through his struggle with high mountains he has learned to acclimatize himself to high altitude conditions. Through subjecting himself to the severest discipline, and preparing himself to endure the hardest hardships and make the costliest sacrifices, he has developed a capacity for living at higher heights. He has become more accustomed to the conditions which prevail there, and invented a technique and an equipment for dealing with them. He has become more familiar with the mountains, till now he is more at home with the Himalayan heights than he was with the Alps before De Saussure climbed Mont Blanc.

And as he has become more at ease among the Himalayan giants, and been able to collect himself and sum up his experiences, he has felt something in the mountains corresponding with something in himself. The more profoundly he has meditated on this the deeper has grown the correspondence. And the deeper the correspondence has grown the more overwhelming has been the beauty which he beholds.

The beauty on the face of the mountains is but the outward expression of the Motive Power at work in the heart of the world. And to put himself in ever-increasing intimacy of communion with this Fountain Source of Things will, from that time forth, be his constant endeavour.

The creature's struggle for mere existence will then be over and his true life have begun. Man will begin to feel the connection and continuity of his own life with the life of Nature, and to see the real universe behind the universe of outward appearance. He will seek to deepen this sense of unity with Nature, and as he succeeds so will his joy increase : he will feel himself exalted to a higher order of being.

Thus will he take the challenge of Everest to heart, and in his own due time give a seemly answer.

Chapter X

A HIMALAYAN PILGRIMAGE

ESPECIALLY by Hindus is this sense of unity with Nature most acutely felt. And to a Hindu the Himalaya is not a playground: it is holy ground. The Himalaya is as holy to Hindus as the Holy Land is to Christians. For thousands of years their profoundest thinkers have found its deep recesses suitable ground for meditation and the practice of spiritual exercises. There they have attained to knowledge of the Absolute and realized God. The most revered saints have had their abode in its recesses. And to this day thousands of pilgrims from all over India every year follow the sacred Ganges to the sacred shrines near its source. They have been taught from their childhood that a river which can bring fertility to the parched-up plains of India must have issued from some divine source. Those who, in ages past, sought its source found it amidst the most impressive mountains. Those gleaming summits of the world must indeed be the dwelling-place of gods. Himalaya—"the abode of snow"—must be the abode of gods. All was holy ground. And they who ventured there must go as pilgrims.

So an Indian venturer into the fastnesses of the Himalaya goes not to test his powers against some Himalayan giant. He thinks not of the attainment of some physical height. He would win the heights of the spirit.

Of these pilgrims I will tell of two, from one of whom, Swami Purohit, author of *An Indian Monk*, I have heard much of the other, Bhagwan Shri Hamsa, the author of *The Holy Mountain*. Both are inhabitants of Western India, yet both have a passion for the Himalaya, more than a thousand miles distant. Like thousands of pilgrims, they have deemed it a privilege to tread in the footsteps of the Mahatmas—the " great souls "—of the past, to be where they had seen the great visions and been inspired to write the great message. But like only a few among these pilgrims they had truly loved the beauties around them, and Swami Purohit has often declared to me his longing to go there once more, to live in a little hut on the banks of the Ganges, spend his days in meditation, and, if God willed, die there.

What these really spiritual pilgrims love is to rise at dawn, bathe, and then in that time of quiet, meditate long and deeply. Hours and hours they will spend in this serene meditation. Every beauty of the forest and the snow-clad mountains and the glorious sky they enjoy. And in the calm of dawn and eventide they will feel the spirit of the Himalaya entering deeply into them.

Bhagwan Shri Hamsa was the elder of the two by

four years. And at the time of the great pilgrimage now to be described he was thirty years of age, and therefore in the prime of life for Himalayan travel. He was slim and athletic, of great beauty and striking personality. Swami Purohit had fallen in love with him at first sight, and has remained ever since his faithful disciple. He was of an intensely spiritual disposition, peculiarly sensitive to impressions. To even the subtlest impressions made upon him by Nature or by man he was most exquisitely susceptible and responsive. And though he was born of wealthy parents, in a good social position, he yet abandoned wealth and position, wife and comfort, to lead the wandering life of a recluse.

Both he and Swami Purohit were devotees of the special god of Western India, the Lord Dattatreya, who is regarded by the Hindus in some way as a god, and in some way as a man—as a god who has become man, or a man who has become god. And he is sometimes spoken of by them as the Lord Dattatreya, and sometimes as Shri Sadguru. For four years Bhagwan Shri Hamsa had travelled in the Himalaya on pilgrimage to the sacred spots at the source of the Ganges—to Kedarnath, Badrinath, and Gangotri. He had known what cold and heat, snow and rain, and lack of food and shelter meant. But through all an ideal had been burning within him. He was determined to see his divine Master, the Lord Dattatreya, on Mount Kailas, the sacred mountain at the back of the Himalaya, in Tibet.

He left Bombay on April 4, 1908, and travelled by train to Bareilly and Kathagodam, from whence he rode to Almora. Here, and on his journey through the lesser ranges, he enjoyed the fresh breeze, the calm nights, the beauty of the forest and the mountain; and a flood of bliss would spring up in his heart such as those alone know who are accustomed to meditate upon God.

At the Ashram of Mayavati, founded by disciples of Swami Vivekenanda for the benefit of those who would lead a life of meditation in the Himalaya, he made the final preparations for his great journey over the Himalaya into Tibet. It is a fitting place from which to start on such a pilgrimage. Situated at an elevation of about 7,000 feet on a wooded ridge, it commands glorious views of the great snowy range. And our pilgrim spent hours a day in serene meditation or in roaming under the stately deodars, admiring the beauties of Nature about him. There was, too, in the Ashram opportunity for study, as it possesses a library of sacred literature and religious periodicals, and publishes a monthly philosophical and religious organ, the *Prabudda Bharata*.

The month he spent here was one of great spiritual refreshment, and on the night before he left he sat long in meditation. His body was weak, but his will was resolute and firm. He had faith in his master, Shri Sadguru. And he had faith in himself. He was sure he would gain his ideal. After his meditation he felt fresh with a strength that could conquer the Himalaya.

He would carry his ideal aloft and be divinely reckless in its pursuit.

Travelling on foot, and taking with him two servants carrying a parcel of biscuits, some tins of condensed milk, candles, and other necessaries, he started for Tibet, making for the valley of the Kali Ganga River, which separates Kumaon from Nepal. His custom was to rise before dawn, perform his religious ceremonies, and make a very early start. Sometimes he would sleep in a house, but he always preferred to lie under the sky rather than be huddled with others in a dirty, dingy travellers' shelter or in a peasant's cottage where "the fleas were too violently active" for him to get any sleep, and from which would exude "a foul stink of flesh and drink."

At Garbiyang, 10,000 feet, at the junction of the Kali Ganga and the Tinker, he stayed for twenty days, and this was evidently a part of his journey which he enjoyed most. On the day he arrived there he had started at 3 a.m., and at 6 a.m. had reached the summit of the ridge above the town. The air was cool. Streams of clear water rushed down the forest-covered mountain-side. All Nature was balmy. An exquisite joy surged within him. He seemed alone in the world, but at one with Nature.

He bathed in a stream. Then he spread his tiger's skin on a large stone slab and, sitting on it, adopted the yogic posture suitable for meditation. The sun was just rising. "The Goddess of Morn, clad in crimson cloth with blue bodice, eagerly awaited the arrival of the Lord ; dewdrops on the grass were shining like pearls ; the mountain peaks seemed to vie with one another in welcoming the glories of the sun ; and the song of birds added music to the charm."

Before he actually commenced his meditation he took one look round on all this. Then the silence and repose and the ineffable beauty of the scene began to bear him aloft. His mind became calm and serene. He fixed the centre of vision between the eyebrows in accordance with yogic practice. Soon he was wrapped in meditation. He became unconscious of the body. He was in the sacred land of spirit, where all was love and bliss.

On his arrival at Garbiyang he found at the confluence of the rivers a quiet spot for meditation to which he would daily resort. It was beyond compare. Snow-clad mountains rose before him, delighting his eye with their grandeur. Below him were tall forests and waving fields of green. His eyes unceasingly feasted on these wonders of Nature. His ears were ravished in the combined song of the birds and rush of the streams. Passing clouds created lovely pictures of colour, light and shade. He was rapt in adoration.

One day after his daily meditation was over, while he was gazing at a bird singing and hopping from bough to bough, the adorative mood suddenly rose within him. He passed into rapture. No tongue can describe his joy. It can be known only to those who have experienced this inexpressible bliss.

So he affirmed. And they who have had experiences

similar to these which he was now enjoying in the midst of the Himalaya, whether they be Indian or European, Christian or Hindu, are convinced of the ultimate goodness of things. They are convinced that a world which can bring such entrancing ecstasy of delight must in its fundamental nature be good.

They are aware of the evil in the world. They may themselves have known something of famine, cholera, plague, earthquakes, wars, animosities, jealousies, theft, craft, and guile. But in the great summing-up of things, even these evils may appear as only transient in the long-run, and to sink into utter insignificance in comparison with the immensity of the good. To them all evil, however great, may appear as something passing, to be infinitely exceeded, surpassed, and redeemed by the overwhelming power for good at work in the heart of the world.

When they return to ordinary workaday life grey doubts may assail them. They may think at times that this conviction of the essential goodness of the world was due only to a wave of emotionalism. Yet even then a more careful reflection may assure them that, though reason alone may never have been able to lead them to this belief as to the ultimate nature of things, their conclusion may still be true. For there may be a higher and truer kind of conviction than can ever be reached by reason alone. There may be a conviction due to a satisfaction, not only of the reason but of the personality as a whole—of intellect, feeling, will, all combined. And their conviction may be of this higher kind. And if this were so, it would be unreasonable to distrust it, and reasonable to trust it. It really may be founded on a great deal more than mere emotionalism. And they may be perfectly justified in staking their lives on its truth and validity, as these Hindu pilgrims do.

Our pilgrim stayed for twenty days at Garbiyang, and then started for Taklakot, in Tibet, by way of the "Tinker Dhura." The pass was 18,000 feet high, and covered with snow. But the sublimity and grandeur of the view from the summit made him cast aside all thoughts of bodily discomfort. He was instantly reminded of the chapter in the *Bhagavad-Gita*, where Krishna showed Arjuna the Cosmic Revelation. He could understand the feelings of a soul which had left this body and been transported to Heaven.

Descending into Tibet, he found the people wild and turbulent, and very suspicious. Any foreign traveller among them must be in constant dread of losing his life. Taklakot was hot in the daytime, but bitingly cold at night. Replenishing his stock of provisions he proceeded on towards Kailas. He was now on the Tibetan plateau, 16,000 feet above sea-level. Bitter winds blew, and, to counteract them, he put on thick clothes, but "they were full of little insects, special products of Tibet, which used to bite like fleas." "Outside was fierce cold," he said, "inside were these insects: we were doubly harassed."

Yet, as always, the Swami had his consolation in the beauty of Nature. Near Kardamkhar he came upon an extensive plain with neither shrub, tree, nor spring to relieve the eye. " All round mountains stood like grim sentinels. It was the hour of sunrise, when the glorious Lord of the Day was appearing over the eastern horizon. All was tranquil. The ice-tipped mountain summits reflected the ruddy rays of the sun and shone like burnished moulds of copper. And no sound of birds could be heard to break the calm repose. We marched slowly along, awed by the grandeur of this scene."

Often at night he would have to sleep in the open, though he would wake covered with snow. Then, at dawn, with his blanket caught tightly about him, he would gaze upon the scene around him. All would be calm and quiet. On the one side were the snow-clad mountains ; on the other stretched the vast plains of Tibet. The sky might be overcast with clouds, but here and there the twinkling of a star would break through. The sight would create in his soul queer ripples of joy. He would be lost in an ocean of bliss. Only those who have experienced it can know the rapture that was his.

At length he came to Lake Rakastal, the source of the river Sutlej, and beyond it he could see Mount Kailas, faint and hazy, in the distance. His Tibetan guide stood as if turned to stone. For full five minutes he remained in prayer, and entreated the Swami to do the same. Arrived on the shores of the lake, the Swami washed his hands, feet, and face, turned towards the cherished object of his journeyings, and in the exaltation of the moment forgot the worry and exhaustion of the journey and all the physical and mental suffering he had endured.

Later in the afternoon Lake Manas came in view, and at the sight of this sacred lake all bowed themselves, with eyes overflowing with joy. For fifteen minutes they remained in adoration, not a word passing from their lips. With Kailas in front, Lake Rakastal to the left, Lake Manas to the right, and the great mountain Gorla Mandhata behind, the scene was truly magnificent. This was indeed holy ground. Lake Manas was the abode of peace. It was the very heart of Nature. The whole region seemed to be not of this earth, but of Heaven. It was the blessed land of the soul. The Swami was lost in rapture as he ever was in face of the glories of Nature. He could find no words to describe the image of God wrought in the Universe—the glory of the cosmic body of Shri Narayen.

For twelve days, during which he was under vow not to speak, he remained on the shores of Lake Manas. He fasted the whole day up till eleven at night, taking only tea. And he engrossed himself in seeking after the Real, Absolute, Eternal Spirit.

After this twelve days of fast and meditation he set out on his pilgrimage round Mount Kailas, and hearing that a great Mahatma lived in a cave on the mountain, he determined to see him. There was no path to the cave, but he longed passionately to have a sight of the Mahatma, and the greater the difficulties in the way of reaching him the stronger grew his resolution. Climbing like a monkey he reached the mouth of the cave. Inside all was dark, and he hesitated before entering. Then he threw himself in, stumbled against something, and in the faint light perceived a human figure. It was the Mahatma.

He was a serene and noble figure, sitting in a yogic posture on a tiger-skin. The Swami bowed in loving adoration before him, praying, " Bless me. Bless me," and was lost in an ecstasy of joy. As he came to see more of him, the Swami found that the Mahatma possessed a tall, stout, hard, comely body. His face seemed to be the abode of serenity, joy, and peace, and to be a veritable fountain of love. His complexion was white. His nose was sharp and aquiline, and his eyes seemed to concentrate in them all the radiance of the Universe. In spite of the cold, he was naked. No ashes covered his body. A bowl and a tiger-skin were his only possessions.

The Swami remained in the company of the Mahatma for three days, during all of which time the latter sat in the same posture day and night, and lived only on water. Every day they conversed together. Whenever the Swami looked at the Mahatma he was absorbed in Divine Bliss, and the Swami was convinced that he was a complete master of the powers of yoga, and one who knew Brahma. The Mahatma was, in the Swami's view, one of those who work for the welfare of the world in the solitude of the recesses of Nature, and often bring about astounding results, though they come into the world unknown and pass out of it unknown.

On the fourth day, early in the morning, the Swami was ordered to depart, and he made his way to Lake Gaurikund. He had to pass over ice, and the cold became so intense that his fingers, nose, and face grew red, and breathing was painfully hard. He felt his limbs swelling, his nerves bursting, and his lips becoming green and blue. But he reached the lake at last, and then the object which he had cherished for so many years was fulfilled.

He had long desired to have a sight of the physical form of the Lord Dattatreya himself, and to get himself initiated into realization of the Self. He would rather die in meditation than not achieve this realization. So now he began his special meditation. He first gazed at the sky and at Mount Kailas. Then he sat on his tiger-skin in a yogic posture with his face towards the north. The sun set. He closed his eyes and passed into meditation, fixing his mind steadily on a mental image of the Lord Dattatreya in the centre between his eyebrows. He experienced terrible hardships—bitter cold, piercing winds, snow, hunger, solitude. Three days and nights he spent in meditation, and during this time lost consciousness of his body and of the world outside him. At last, all of a sudden, the mental form of the Lord Dattatreya disappeared. His eyes were opened, and there, standing before him, was the lord, in his physical form. The Swami prostrated himself before his Master, and his Master lifted him up to His breast, caressed him all over, and initiated him into the realization of the Self. The Swami's joy was indescribable. His mind was merged into his heart, and all was merged into the absolute Brahma. He found himself reflected everywhere in the Universe. All was one harmony, full of Infinite Wisdom, Perennial Love, and Bliss Eternal.

On the evening of the fourth day the Swami returned to his camp, and on the next day met another Mahatma with the same sweet voice, the same peace and serenity of features, and the same Divine Light beaming from his eyes as the Mahatma in the cave had displayed. The Swami then proceeded to Gartok, in Western Tibet, and from there returned to India by the way he had entered Tibet.

Once more he found himself on the forests of the lower Himalayan ranges, where Nature puts on her best dress. His eyes devoured the luxurious verdure, so delicious after the barren plains of Tibet. Once again he was travelling alongside the Ganges. He walked ahead of his coolies, humming and musing to himself as joy welled up in his heart. Beneath a tree he halted and gazed on the sacred river flowing serenely below him. Suddenly he was lost in the ecstasy of meditation, and flew into the Land of the Soul.

At Almora he remained for a fortnight, and thoroughly recovered his health. Then he travelled on to Bombay, which he reached on 11th October. He had been six months and seven days on his pilgrimage, and spent on it one hundred and seventy-five rupees.

With prayers to the Almighty that the Sun of Glory might ever shine on his Motherland and her children, and on the Eternal Religion, he asks the gentle reader to accept his story. From love it had proceeded. And with love he would wish it received.

Chapter XI

HOLY HIMALAYA

THUS have the Hindus, for thousands of years, regarded the Himalaya as holy ground. They are by nature a religiously disposed people. To them it seemed that those sublime heights could only be the abode of gods. So they have built shrines both where the sacred Ganges issues from the mountains and at its glacier source in the deep heart of the Himalaya. And to these shrines, as we have seen, thousands of Hindus make pilgrimage.

Nor are these pilgrims simple, superstitious villagers only. Among them are Brahmins of the highest culture, like the pilgrim in the last chapter, who recall the glorious literature which has been inspired by the mountains, and who would fain tread in the hallowed footsteps of those who had felt so deeply. Renouncing all worldly possessions, severing all family ties, Hindus of the highest intellectual eminence and recognized social position will delight in making the pilgrimage. They will cheerfully endure incredible hardships from rain, frost, ice, and snow in order that, in the depths of the Himalaya, their hearts may be purified and they may experience God. Some of them will pierce through the Himalaya to the sacred mountain of Kailas in Tibet, and there spend months in meditation till they have attained to such a degree of sanctity that holiness positively radiates from them.

Can we Europeans not see in this custom of the Hindus a hint of the spiritual enjoyment which we also might derive from the Himalaya? Might not we, too, regard the Himalaya as holy ground? And might not we also thither ascend? Such pilgrimages would be conducted in a different way from that which Hindus follow. But they may be none the less effective in bringing the pilgrims into contact with the Primal Source of Things, and in enabling them to experience for once in a lifetime that intensity of enjoyment which such contact infallibly brings. Through a deepening union with the Spirit of which the mountains are but the symbols and outward manifestations, the European pilgrims may experience that ineffable bliss of which the Hindu sages, modern as well as ancient, have always told.

Where, then, in the Himalaya, should be our places of pilgrimage? The Hindus sought the source of their sacred river, and made that spot the object of their pilgrimage. We would be animated by a different desire. Our aim would be to reach that point where mountain makes its deepest impression on man. The Everest climbers took the summit of Everest as the object of their endeavours, because Everest was the highest mountain in the world. Smythe chose Kamet because it was a 25,000-feet peak, and no one had yet climbed a peak of that height. In these and many other such cases the attainment of altitude was the main object. The climbers did not set out for the summit for the sake of the view. Often, when they reached the summit, they were hidden in cloud and had no view at all. Extreme altitude also prevented them from the enjoyment of views they had on the way up. The aim of pilgrims would not therefore be to reach the summit of some high peak only on account of its height. Beauty and not altitude would be their main consideration. Wherever it might be—on a pass, on the crest of some ridge, or on the summit of some minor mountain—they would seek that position where they would be able to see the mountains in the highest perfection of their beauty and see beauty in its greatest variety. And that position would have to be so reasonably accessible that they would be able to reach it in a condition enabling them really to enjoy the view. If it were at such an altitude, for instance, that they would be too exhausted to take in the full beauty of the scene, that position would be useless for their purpose. Also the position must be such that they could remain in it for hours—even for nights—so as to be able, at complete leisure, to absorb every varying element of beauty. What the European pilgrim would seek then is that spot where the Himalaya could make its profoundest impression on him—where he might find deepest correspondence between the spirit in the mountain and the spirit in himself, and so see the full perfection of its beauty.

Photograph by Bentley Beetham.

IN THE TEESTA VALLEY.

To reach that vantage-point severe calls may be made upon his powers of endurance. For it is most desirable that the pilgrim should be able to remain in the open air by night as well as by day, so that he may receive the full benefit of contact with the mountains and with all Nature. He should be independent of house or tent for shelter, be able to set forth on his pilgrimage with only one or two porters to carry food and bedding, and so be free to sleep on the ground under the stars, to climb wherever he needs in search of the best view-point, and to remain there as long as he wishes, night or day. Stamina, therefore, will be essential for the hard physical exertion the pilgrimage will entail. And nerve, too ; for perilous climbing may be required of him.

Then for fully entering into the spirit of the mountains his own spirit must be at its keenest. On arrival at the place of pilgrimage he will have to be taking in every beauty in the scene about him, and to be meditating intently on each, and appreciating its full significance. He will need, therefore, to have trained his mind in searching out essentials and disciplined it in concentration on them. He will need, further, to have learnt what to look for, and how to appreciate the subtlest elements that go to make the beauty of the scene—be able instantly to register and respond to the quickly changing impressions, to detect the delicatest hues and the minutest details in the building of the whole. Then, setting aside all attention to the parts, he will need the capacity to lean back, as it were, and quietly absorb the impression of the whole and let it, in all its greatness, take possession of his soul. And for all this, much mental training, much cultivation of the spirit, and much exercise in appreciation will be required.

In both body and spirit the pilgrim will need to fit himself. And there the experience of the Everest climbers will make itself felt. They were aiming at only the highest physical height. But even for that they had to fit themselves to the topmost pitch in spirit as well as in body. Manifestly, they had to have their bodies at their very fittest, every muscle at its tautest, every internal organ functioning at perfection, or they would never be able to stand the appalling strain to which they would be subjected from cold, from lack of oxygen, and from dangerous climbing on ice and rock. Nowhere is a severer strain put upon the human organism than upon an Everest climber on the last day of his climb. And it is not only his body that is tried to the extreme : his spirit also is put to the test. He might be of perfect physique and in the very pink of condition, but if he had not the courage to endure the piercing blizzards, the nerve to tread undaunted the very edge of ghastly precipices, and the will to press onward when death-like lethargy was settling on him, he would never reach the summit. An Everest climber must be fit in spirit as well as in body. And if such perfection of spirit as well as of body is needed for the attainment of the highest physical height, how much more necessary must it be for the attainment of the loftiest spiritual eminence ?

These, then, are the required capacities and preparation of a pilgrim. He must take his pilgrimage no less seriously than does the Everest climber his expedition to Everest. Then, with body inured to hardship, and healthy with the health of the open air, his mind and soul will be able to devote themselves to the main object of his pilgrimage. And as the bodies of Everest climbers acclimatize themselves to higher and higher physical heights, so will the pilgrim's soul acclimatize itself to the higher and ever higher heights of the spirit, till it is able to endure the extremest demands which are made upon it, and by concentrating the mind first on one element and then on another, and then on all in their togetherness, appreciate to the full the perfection of the whole.

Where, then, in the Himalaya should the pilgrim go in order to obtain from the mountains the full impression of their greatness ? Where shall be the Mountain Sanctuaries of the future ? The Hindus, for centuries past, have had their places of pilgrimage fixed. The source of the Ganges, or the cave of Amarnath in Kashmir, are well established, and the Hindu pilgrim has only to choose which of them most appeals to him. For the European pilgrim in search of mountain beauty the places of pilgrimage are not yet fixed. He knows within a yard or two the exact position of the highest physical heights. But no survey of the Himalaya as a whole has yet been made to determine those points at which a pilgrim might obtain the highest elevation of the soul. The selection of Mountain Sanctuaries is the great work which still remains to be done. Visitors to the Himalaya have, of course, roughly indicated certain points from which they have seen specially beautiful views of the mountains. But they have paid no special attention to deliberately searching round till they have discovered the exact position from which a mountain, or a range, may be seen to its best advantage. And that is what must now be done. We must pay attention to the beauty of the Himalaya and determine where that may best be seen. We must choose our Sanctuaries.

In my Presidential Address to the Royal Geographical Society, in 1920, I propounded the revolutionary doctrine that geographers should regard the earth as mother-earth, and the beauty of her features as just as much within the purview of geography as their altitude and exact location. As geographers, we were concerned with the face and features of the earth, and the characteristic of the face and features of the earth most worth learning about, knowing, and understanding, was their beauty. And the reason why it was most worth knowing about was because beauty is a quality which appeals to the universal in man, appeals to all men for all time, and appeals to men in an increasing degree. I therefore urged that the Society should encourage the search for natural beauty, and look upon the discovery of a new region which possessed special beauty, or the discovery of a new beauty in a region already well known, as among the most important geographical discoveries to be made.

I would now plead that this notion should be applied to the Himalaya in particular. Of this most prominent feature on the face of mother-earth we should be enabled to appreciate the full beauty. And for this purpose a deliberate survey should be made to determine where are those points from which the beauty of the Himalaya may best be seen—where are the Sanctuaries to which pilgrims might make their pilgrimage. Such a survey would be the work of many men for many years. But in time certain spots will come to be recognized as suitable goals for a pilgrimage, and at them Mountain Sanctuaries might gradually be established and consecrated for ever to the worship of Beauty.

Already we do know approximately where to search for the best view-points. Survey officers, travellers, explorers, climbers, have by now penetrated to most parts of the Himalaya. And though Beauty has not been the main object of these journeyings, they have, in the course of their travels, been struck at certain places by the special grandeur of the scene. The neighbourhood of those might be systematically searched for spots on which men might best be able to receive the full impress of the mountains.

Darjiling is the best-known of these view-points. From Darjiling, the view of Kangchenjunga is of such world-wide celebrity that it need only be referred to here. But, famous as it is, other points might well be sought from which the great mountain might be seen from different angles—side face, three-quarter face, as well as full face. Away in the direction of Nepal, too, along the Sangalila ridge, magnificent views may be obtained of Everest and Makalu, as well as of Kangchenjunga. And in the other direction, in Sikkim, there is great scope for ascents of spurs and ridges in search of profile views of Kangchenjunga.

Farther west is Nepal. It is forbidden country to Europeans, but perhaps the Nepalese themselves might engage in search for view-points. The southern half of Everest is situated in Nepal. And from some ridge facing it there must be superb views of that tremendous southern face which plunges down so precipitously into the glacier valley below. Then there must be terrific gorges in Nepal, as where the Arun River, rising in Tibet, bursts through the Himalaya. Magnificent scenery there must be, if only the Nepalese would tell us of it, and at least bring photographs to give us some faint inkling ; for, according to Kenneth Mason, there are in Nepal three known summits over 27,000 feet in height, seven over 26,000, and fourteen over 25,000. Nepal must be a paradise of great peaks.

Moving farther northward and westward we come to the British district of Kumaon, with the hill-stations of Almora and Ranikhet. Here all is freely accessible. And as, before the monsoon breaks, it is free of the constant rain which makes sleeping-out in the Kang-

Photograph by F. S. Smythe.

THE ALAKNANDA VALLEY

chenjunga area so undesirable, pilgrimages might be made without tents, and the whole paraphernalia of camp furniture. Here, and for the rest of the Himalaya northward, from April to July and from the end of September onward, clear, fine weather is the rule. Tents are by no means a necessity, and more often a nuisance. A hill-man or two would carry all that was necessary. And the pilgrim might devote the whole of his energies and his thought to his one quest of the best view-point.

This part of the Himalaya I have never visited, but I can remember Lord Curzon's enthusiasm over it and his pleasure that it was so accessible. Those who have crossed the Kuari Pass have spoken with awe and delight of the views from there of the 25,000-feet peaks. But no one, so far as I know, has settled down there for some weeks and designedly set to work to explore the whole ridge in search of the finest vantage-point. The beauties of the Nanda Devi basin have been described by Oliver and Shipton. And Marco Pallis tells of an ideal spot for a base camp, Khyarkuti, near Harsil, a meeting-place of several deep glens, each affording a glimpse into a fine glacier basin with its dominating peaks. Here, then, is a good field for beauty exploration.

Simla is situated on the ridge which divides the waters which flow into the Indus and so into the Arabian Sea, from those which flow into the Ganges and so into the Bay of Bengal. And expeditions might be made along that ridge in the direction of Tibet to find the best points from which the snowy range on the opposite side of the Sutlej valley may be seen. None of the really great views of the Himalaya will be found there. Yet fine mountains are to be seen. And points of pilgrimage may be found reasonably accessible for those who can get away for even a few days from the hard work of the Government offices and the strenuous gaieties of Simla, and really desire to refresh and replenish their souls.

Kulu is a most beautiful country of the Alpine order of magnitude. Rich forests clothe the mountain-sides. The people are cheerful and of good looks. And the climate is perfect. View-points might certainly here be found where the more quiet glories of the Himalaya might be enjoyed.

Kashmir does not possess so superb a view of the Himalaya as that seen from Darjiling ; but second only to that is some of the scenery at the back of Kashmir. And with a perfect climate the exploring for view-points may be carried out under ideal conditions. And among these peaks the first to mark is Nanga Parbat, 26,620 feet in altitude, which lies immediately behind the valley, and which might be taken as a focal point for many explorations. Standing apart by itself, above all other peaks in its neighbourhood, it may be seen from many different directions, and view-points of it are readily accessible. To find these would, in itself, be a worthy object for a whole series of expeditions.

From as far away as the Murree ridge overlooking the plains of the Punjab it is visible. From Gulmarg, looking right across the Valley of Kashmir and over the Wular Lake, it may be seen dominating the whole valley. At close quarters there must be many magnificent positions from which to view it amid the ranges on the northern side of the valley. Then on the far side of the mountain, from a ridge behind Gilgit, may be had a view of it which for conveying an impression of sheer altitude is the finest known. The observer from this point, at a height of 10,000 feet above sea-level, looks down into the Indus valley, here only 3,300 feet, and from there straight up to Nanga Parbat, 26,620 feet. Over 23,000 feet of mountain in a single rise without any intervening ridges.

From that same standpoint may also be seen, though at some distance, Rakapushi in Hunza, 25,000 feet in height. And view-points of this magnificent mountain might be another object of search. It is more of a massif than a peak, and is of most majestic appearance as seen from the Hunza valley. There must in Hunza and Nagar, and in the Gilgit district, be many points on the mountains opposite to it from which more impressive views of it might be obtained.

Remoter still, in the mountains behind Kashmir, is that wonderful region of the Baltoro Glacier which culminates in the great peak K_2, 28,250 feet in height, the second highest mountain in the world, even the satellites of which reach altitudes of 27,000 and 26,000 feet. And, remotest of all, and only reached with the greatest difficulty, and after long marches, is the region beyond that again—the region on the far side of the Karakoram range beyond the watershed of India and Central Asia. In this far, uninhabited, and barely explored region, at the very foot of K_2 and the Gusherbrum peaks on the north, may be obtained views of surpassing grandeur. It is my pride to have been the first European to visit this region. And it has since been explored by Kenneth Mason, the Duke of Spoleto's Expedition, and now, in 1935, by the indefatigable Dutch explorer, Dr. Visser. But none of us has specially explored it for the purpose of discovering those points in that region of rock and ice beyond all vegetation and all human habitation from which the great peaks may be viewed to best advantage. We have seen them from the passes and the valleys, but we have not deliberately sought out the finest view-points. That is the greatest enterprise which remains to be accomplished. All that stern region, both south and north of the line of great peaks, has to be definitely explored in order to discover those spots to which the hardiest pilgrims may make their pilgrimage to obtain an impression of mountain majesty at its very grandest.

In such regions—there and thereabout—will be found scenery of a scale and character to be found nowhere else in the world. But in other parts of the Himalaya, and in those parts which lie on the way to the loftier regions, will be found scenery of the European order, such as is found in Switzerland. And those returning from the greater heights appreciate and enjoy these gentler glories all the more as a relief from their severer journeyings. And for the benefit of those who have it not in their power to go farther, there are in these less lofty regions many places suitable for spiritual pilgrimage.

Kashmir is renowned for its beauty. The valley is about eighty miles long and twenty-five miles wide. Through it runs in measured flow the river Jhelum. It abounds in clumps of the umbrageous oriental plane tree. The villages are surrounded with mulberry trees, and in spring with purple irises; and dotted over the valley are lakes of dreamy loveliness. But what constitutes the special beauty of Kashmir is that it is surrounded on every side by snowy mountains. In whatever direction one looks the eye is met by a snowy range—north and south, east and west, the landscape is closed by lines of snowy peaks not too close to be overpowering, and not too far to be indistinguishable. In the spring, when the trees are covered with the freshest green, when innumerable apricot, pear, and apple trees are in bloom, and fields of yellow mustard and blue flax are glowing with colour, and the delicatest purply haze merges into the azure of the sky, we think that nothing could be lovelier on earth. But in the autumn, when the air has been washed by the monsoon rains, when the sky is clean and clear, and there is a sparkle in the sunshine, and the whole valley is ablaze with the gold and reds and browns of the autumn foliage on the planes and poplars, and we know for certain that for weeks to come there will be day after day of unfailing sunshine and crisp, cool air, we wonder if even spring can equal this autumnal glory.

Then on the mountain-sides are rich primeval forests of the stately deodar, silver fir, blue pine, spruce, maple, horse chestnut, walnut, sycamore, and, on the higher edges, silver birch. The mountain meadows are rich with alpine flowers, white and purple columbines, delphiniums, yellow violets, balsams, mauve and yellow primulas, potentillas, anemones, Jacob's ladder, monks-hood, salvia, and many, many other plants. Looking through these forests out over the valley beneath, over the winding river and the placid Wular Lake, and over the range of the Alpine order of magnitude which bounds the valley on the north, we catch a view of the wonderful Nanga Parbat, 10,000 feet higher than any European mountain. And here amidst the ferns and flowers, in perfect ease and comfort, the pilgrim may be able to collect his whole mind and direct it undistracted to the one main object of appreciating and absorbing the varied beauties round him.

From any hill-stations along the outlying spurs of the Himalaya from Darjiling through Masouri, to Dharmsala and Murree, spots may be found to which these more generally feasible pilgrimages might periodically be taken by those who have not the time or the physical capacity to go farther. Many travellers and sojourners in the Himalaya may be too young or too old, too poor or too frail to climb the great peaks, but may yet be true mountaineers. They may have a true love of the mountains and be as able as any Everest climber to enter into the real spirit of the mountains. And these would like to know of spots where they may snatch a few precious moments from the swirl and scurry of life to put themselves in touch with the inner heart of things and find comfort for their souls.

While on his pilgrimage the pilgrim might seek occasions for entering into the life, not only of the trees and flowers, but of the animals also. In the lower parts of Sikkim the insect life is too intrusive to admit of quiet meditation, but even this is recompensed by the beauty of the butterflies of every gorgeous or most delicate hue. And elsewhere, above the line of insect pests, animal life of many kinds may be found, and graceful deer, the majestic Kashmir stag, the alert ibex, and all the vivid life of birds be gratefully observed.

To know this animal and tree and flower life the better, the pilgrim would do well to seek out two men—a Sportsman and a Forest Officer. And the sportsman should be the true sportsman—a man, like Colonel Ward of Kashmir, who loves to pit his own skill and sagacity, his endurance and courage against the alertness of the stag or the ibex, or the ferocity of the bear or the tiger; and who for years has studied the ways and nature of the game he pursues. And the Forest Officer may be a naturalist as well as an official. If so, besides his knowledge of the trees in his care and the way to preserve his forest, he will have love for the wild life of all kinds amidst which he spends his somewhat lonely days.

With his intimate knowledge of the forest world in which he may have lived for years, he will be able to penetrate a little into the deep mystery of this silent but intense life of the forest, and understand how flowers and insects, trees and birds and animals all interact with one another to form one harmonious whole. He might tell of life feeding on life—as the thrush feeds on the worm on an English lawn, or as he would find microbe feeding on microbe in his own body if he could see his interior with a microscope. He might tell of the fittest surviving in the struggle, and the unfit being mercilessly dispatched. But he would tell also of mutual aid, both conscious and unconscious, of combinations against aggressors, and of the heroism of mothers in the protection of their young. And even of birds of prey he might tell of their maternal solicitude as well as of their keenness of eye, their swiftness of swoop, and deftness in execution. And he would assuredly affirm the *joie de vivre* of the life in the forest. As we may also observe here in England, wild life is not, in the main, a life of fear and tribulation. Cruelty and suffering there are. But, perforce, the life is one of vigour and vigilance. All living things are kept keyed-up. They are at the top of their being. Cries of distress may sometimes be heard ; but the overwhelming note is of joy.

With the cheerful peoples of the Himalaya, gayer than the peoples of the plains, the pilgrim might also put himself in contact. In engaging porters he might find that there are bad lots among them as among other peoples. There are pilferers and sluggards, and those who drink and stay up late at night, and are consequently late at starting in the morning. But if care be taken in the choice of the very few required on a pilgrimage there may be found those who may be treated on a very much higher footing than mere carriers of equipage—men who may be treated as the Everest climbers treated their best porters, as real comrades. And many of these are religious at heart. We have seen how the Everest porters liked getting the blessing of lamas, and showed a truly religious spirit. As I have previously told, often on some critical occasion, or when a danger is over, I have seen Himalayan peoples show a deep-seated sense of dependence on some unseen Power behind things. Such men would thoroughly enter into the spirit of the pilgrimage and could be treated as fellow-pilgrims.

Lastly—and this is a new and important suggestion—deliberate efforts might be made to get into contact with those most spiritual Indians who come to the Himalaya from all parts of India on the pilgrimage of their lifetime—and also with those of them who remain in the Himalaya in ashrams or as priests of temples. These might be met on spiritual grounds, and they would well appreciate the ardour with which the European pilgrim admired the glories of the Himalaya.

The priest of the temple at Ukimath was most kind in his attentions to Shipton's Expedition in 1934. "We were received," says Shipton, "with a hospitality which will live long among my most cherished memories." At Badrinath they received as warm a welcome from another spiritual Hindu, Ram Serikh Singh, who was once professor of philosophy in an Indian university, but who had now retired to spend the summer months in solitary contemplation in the beautiful glens near Badrinath. He was an imposing figure and a lover of the mountains, and had travelled extensively and made the pilgrimage round the holy peak of Kailas, in Tibet. He had boundless knowledge of the history and mythology of this sacred part of the Himalaya. And he was kind enough to spend a whole evening with the climbers discoursing on these things.

This priest, who came from the south of India, and this Swami are typical of hundreds of highly-cultured Indians who are attracted to the Himalaya by its sacred traditions. There are also in the Himalaya communities like the Ashram at Mayavate, near Almora, founded by Swami Vivekenanda, which are given over to the contemplation of spiritual truth and beauty. European pilgrims would only have to treat these spiritual Indians with the courtesy which is their due, and with their innate Indian grace they would eagerly respond. They would rejoicingly welcome those who, like themselves, had been attracted thither by the glory of the mountains. And they would revel in converse on their sublimity.

From these men much light on the way in which Hindus regard the Himalaya might be obtained. And

Photograph by the Everest Flight.

MAKALU FROM THE AIR.

if the European pilgrims were to get into touch, soul to soul, with these Indian aspirants after spiritual heights, and also sympathetically interest themselves in the religious ceremonials and festivals, the music, and the dancing, and the ways of looking at life of these Indian pilgrims, a spiritual fellowship of the Himalaya might insensibly spring up which would add inestimably to the joy of pilgrimage for all concerned. Between these pilgrims to the heights would be the common bond of a single aspiration. Everest might well be the symbol of the fellowship, and its practice a reverent worship of all that is most high and pure and lovely wherever found.

Pilgrimages such as we have contemplated to the selected Mountain Sanctuaries might be made sometimes by pilgrims in the very prime of life, able to penetrate to the remotest and loftiest Sanctuaries, and sometimes by those past the prime or otherwise unfitted or unable to proceed farther than to the nearer and lower places of pilgrimage. But in all cases the pilgrim, by making sustained effort to concentrate his attention on the beauties at hand, and by meditating earnestly on their perfection, might attain to some degree of spiritual enjoyment. Each pilgrim might fit and train himself to the full measure of his capacity. Then, having chosen the holy place of pilgrimage to which he will make his way, he will set his whole heart upon getting the fullest spiritual enjoyment from his pilgrimage—from the forests he will pass through, from the forest life he may observe, from the companionship of the Himalayan people he may have to employ, from fellow-pilgrims he may meet on the way, and finally from the beauty at the goal of his pilgrimage. And perhaps, if this spot is not too remote—if it is in the lesser ranges and near the ordinary hill-stations—he may be able to return again and again to it till he knows it in every mood.

In this sacred place, wherever it may be, he might well ponder upon the secret of the world. Upon what it really is at bottom, and upon how we are connected with it. Is it only a gigantic machine grinding relentlessly on, crushing us in earthquakes, starving us in famines, killing us in plagues, and eventually extinguishing our lives and all we had so hardly wrought for? Is it a mere mechanical contrivance—that and nothing more? And are we men mere cogs on one of its wheels? Or is it, like the human body, a most exquisitely delicate and intricately constructed machine yet one which is also dominated by mind—one with which we are as intimately connected as each one of the million million million cells of which I am composed is related to me, impressed with the image of me, growing up in that image, remaining a constituent part of me, and taking a part in the shaping of me as I have taken a part in the shaping of it?

We want light upon what is the real nature of the world. Is it to be distrusted and feared? Or can it be trusted and loved? Are we to go through life making the best of a bad job ? Or are we to pass our days with an inward peace, confident that things are well with the world ? In face of the evils and distresses so glaringly evident, this is no easy matter to decide. Yet it is one which each of us should definitely settle to at least his own satisfaction, for upon its solution depends his whole attitude to life. And under what more suitable conditions could he finally compose his soul than in the quietude of a Mountain Sanctuary, while he is at the top of his health ?

CHAPTER XII

STARRY NIGHTS

MAY I be excused for indulging once more in just this final chapter in my favourite pursuit—contemplation of the stars? For to me stars and mountains are inextricably connected, and I cannot write of the mountains without thinking of the stars.

But in reading mountain literature I have been astonished to see how little mention is made of the stars. I have sought the reason, and I believe it to lie in the fact that European mountaineers seldom sleep in the open. They therefore think intensely of the mountain but very little of the stars. In their ordinary life after dusk they are either in their homes or at some indoor place of entertainment. And on Alpine climbs they usually start from and finish their day in an hotel or hut. They seldom lie out in the open. And those European climbers who come to the Himalaya come to climb such very high mountains that they are forced to sleep in tents. Neither in Europe nor in the Himalaya do these mountaineers dwell with the stars. Hence the absence of reference to stars in their writings.

My own experience has not been in climbing the

great peaks of the Himalaya. My time was spent in the humbler task of exploring the valleys and passes. I only viewed the great peaks from the passes. But through being at a lower level I was able to spend my nights in the open. For weeks together I slept night after night under the stars with the mountains round me. So in exploring my way through the mountains I came to have them connected in my mind with the stars. And I was very young and impressionable when I first crossed the entire breadth of the Himalaya, so the impression made by stars and mountains went deep. Moreover, two years later, when I was still only twenty-six, I had to find my way through an unexplored part of the Himalaya by means of nightly observations to the stars for latitude. So my interest in them increased. On my return to civilization I liked to learn more about them. Jeans was not then out of the university, or Eddington out of school. But they had precursors in Norman Lockyer, Procter, Ball, and Flammarion, who used to make astronomy intelligible to us lay seekers after knowledge of the stars. And from them I learned much. But I would not only increase my knowledge: I would deepen my feeling for the stars. Poems like Matthew Arnold's "Self-Dependence," dealing with the influence of stars upon him, profoundly affected me.

Thus it came about that from the time of my night journey across the Gobi Desert in 1887, when seated on a camel, there was little else but the stars to attract my attention, up to the present time, when I can attend

Jeans' or Eddington's lectures, and at scientific meetings hear the latest developments of astronomy discussed, I have always retained my interest in the stars. And now I would like to view in one sweep this influence of nearly fifty years upon me, and recall their connection with the mountains.

First, then, may I briefly re-state the circumstances in which I began to come under the spell of the stars in conjunction with the mountains? It was in 1887, when crossing the Himalaya by an unexplored route. Night after night, at the close of a hard day's tussle with the mountains, I would settle down with my men to an evening meal round the camp-fire, and then, refreshed by dinner and satisfied with myself that one stage farther had been reached, I would compose myself for the night in my sleeping-bag on the bare ground and leisurely regard the stars and the mountains round me. No tent stood between me and them. Their light came directly on me. Thus attuned, I lay and watched the mountains. No longer were they terrible obstacles to be fought against and overcome. No longer were they hard, and stern, and cold. Their very substantiality had disappeared. In the gentle starlight they looked what science now tells us they, in fact, are—utterly ethereal. I was in a different world. Far below me was the distant, murky world in which we ordinarily dwell. I had risen step by step by infinite exertion, and after running many a risk, to a loftier region of spotless purity and of the most entrancing beauty.

There, in the great silence and utter stillness, the

radiance of the stars seemed positively to penetrate me. They shone with a brilliance only known at those great heights. But it was not the brilliance of any single star that pierced. It was the radiance of all in their togetherness which insensibly seeped into me. The whole vault of heaven seemed to shed a benign but most elevating influence on me. And I no longer belonged to earth alone. I was still of the earth, for I was lying on it, in direct bodily contact with it; but I and the mountains and the stars were all bound up together in one whole. And with the sun no longer occupying an undue prominence in the scheme of things, but, for the time being out of the picture, my real position in the universe was much more evident. I belonged to the starry firmament, and not only to the solar system. A truer conception of the universe and of our relation to it began to form itself in my mind.

Then, suggested no doubt by some book I had read, there gradually dawned upon me the idea that some of those myriads of stars, being suns like our own sun, must have planets like our earth, and that on some of those planets must be living beings, very different in outward form from us, but just as intelligent. I had been travelling among very secluded peoples hidden away in remote Himalayan valleys who imagined that the world consisted of only a few other valleys besides their own, inhabited by men much the same as themselves. They had no conception of great civilizations like the Chinese, the Indian, and the European. And as I reflected on this fact I thought that we inhabitants of this planet might be equally narrow in our outlook on the universe. So, forty years ago, I wrote in my *Heart of a Continent*: "Man is the highest form of living being in this single little world of ours—this little speck, which is to the universe as the smallest grain of sand to the stretch of seashore. But is he the highest in the whole universe? Are not the probabilities overwhelmingly in favour of his not being so? Would it not be the veriest chance if, among all these millions of worlds, this one on which we live should have happened to develop the highest being?"

This was pure speculation on my part. But in the intervening years I have carefully noted the progress of astronomy to see how this speculation has increased or decreased in probability. Then I wrote that the number of stars were to be reckoned not by thousands but by millions—by hundreds of millions. Now we reckon them not by hundreds of millions, but by millions of millions. Their number is compared to the number of grains of sand in the Sahara Desert, or on all the seashores of the world. Then I wrote of stars being so distant that light from them, travelling at the rate of 186,000 miles a second, must have started before the birth of Christ, say two thousand years ago. Now nebulæ have been observed through the great telescope on Mount Wilson the light from which must have started 140,000,000 years ago. To this extent has our knowledge of the number of the stars and the magnitude of the physical universe increased during the last forty years. And with this increase of knowledge the increase also of the probability that higher beings than ourselves may exist in the universe.

But this is not all. More important still is our increased knowledge of the ultimate nature of matter, and of what Whitehead calls the connexity of things. Myself reposing on a Himalayan glacier, and the whole starry universe arrayed around me, are connected together to a degree unsuspected forty years ago. Light comes from the stars: there must therefore be some kind of connexion. But it was then supposed that the atoms were the ultimate particles of matter, and that they were something in the nature of minute pellicules. It was not known that each particle of which my body, and the glacier on which I lay, and the mountains round me, was composed, was something so *im*material as to be simply a centre of energy, that the influence of each extended to the confines of the universe, and that the sensitivity of each was so keen that it was influenced by the whole universe—atoms of the inmost iron core of this earth being influenced by and influencing atoms in the nebula 140 million light-years away. This wonderful connexity of things was unrealized in those days.

It was not suspected that in what was then mistakenly termed the "inorganic" world could be found phenomena which were the same as those of life, the atom being, as Dr. J. S. Haldane now shows, "something of which the existence, like that of a living organism, is an expression of ceaseless co-ordinated activity, incapable of being interpreted in mechanical terms as that of a mere particle in the old sense" ; and that, therefore, "life must be regarded as ultimately inherent in what we at present picture as inorganic phenomena."

Now if the ultimate units of which the universe is composed are so all-pervasive in the influence they exert, and so sensitively impressionable to influences from the universe as a whole, and if life is inherent in the universe, has not the probability enormously increased that there are in the universe many planets of many stars on which may dwell living intelligent beings? And is not the probability of there existing intelligent beings further increased if the whole universe is found to be not only a living universe but a universe possessed of personality? What creates difficulty in supposing that beings more intelligent than ourselves exist on other planets in other parts of the universe is the baneful habit we have caught from scientists of regarding the universe as fundamentally material, with life and mind as chance and temporary by-products. But if we acquire an exactly opposite habit and come to look upon mind not as a casual, insignificant by-product, but as the determining factor at the very foundation of things, then the universe will assume a very different aspect. Then it will appear as the most natural thing in the world that this Universal Mind should be continually manifesting itself, on this planet and on that, throughout all space and all time. In which case living, intelligent beings would have existed on other planets of other stars long before they appeared here, and will continue to exist long after life has disappeared from planets of our own particular sun.

And that there is good ground for supposing that mind is thus behind all and through all we may assume if a scientific man of Dr. J. S. Haldane's eminence can hold that the surrounding world of Nature is no mere physico-chemical or even biological world, but a world in which personality is just as much embodied as it is in ourselves—that the scientific aspects are only partial interpretations of the universe, and that the real universe is a manifestation of personality. And we may be reassured in our assumption when we find that this view of a scientific man is shared by most of the leading philosophers of the day.

Those who argue against the probability of life existing on the planets of other stars have pointed to the peculiar conditions under which life exists on this planet—the special chemical elements and their special combinations under special conditions of temperature and moisture. And they have contended that it is extremely unlikely that such special conditions would prevail on any other planet—or at any rate on very few—and therefore that it is highly improbable that life exists anywhere else in the universe than on this planet.

But, as the French astronomer, Camille Flammarion, long ago pointed out, to reason thus is to reason not like a philosopher but like a fish. "Every rational fish ought to assume that it is impossible to live out of water, since its outlook and its philosophy do not extend beyond its daily life." Take one of those fishes which have quite recently been observed 3,000 feet below the surface of the ocean. In those great depths no ray of light penetrates. All is darkness, except for the spots of phosphorescent or electric light which the fishes bear on some parts of their bodies. How could any of those fishes conceive of life in the air and sunshine in which sea-gulls, not a mile above them, are living? It would be against " reason " in the fish to suppose any such thing. Yet there are the sea-gulls—not to mention ocean liners and aeroplanes.

And even when the life is actually being lived before the eyes of certain creatures, they know nothing of it. The butterflies flitting over the hillsides of Palestine nineteen hundred years ago knew nothing of the life which was being preached in the Sermon on the Mount, and lived by the Preacher. The scientific men who doubt the existence of life on other planets may be just as obtuse as the fish and the butterfly.

For all we know the conditions on this planet may be extremely unfavourable for the development of life; and on other planets of other stars the conditions may be far more conducive to the appearance and development of living things. As Bergson suggests, it looks as if whatever matter could be secured here for the embodiment of life was ill-adapted to favour its impetus—ill-adapted, not well-adapted. The process of evolution from amœba to man has taken a prodigiously long time—about a thousand million years. Under more favourable conditions, such as may exist on other planets of other stars, the whole process of evolution might have been vastly superior to what it has been here. In these other planets the matter through which life rushes to embody itself may be less refractory than the matter here. Life may take up other of the known chemical elements than it uses on this planet, and the temperature conditions in which it has to work may be more favourable.

On this earth life fixed its choice mainly upon the carbon of carbonic acid. But on other planets the same result might have been obtained by entirely different means. The essential thing life has to do is to store the energy of the star. Energy is the ultimate constituent of the physical universe ; and the function of life is to store and accumulate this energy and thus canalize it and expend it in variable directions—slowly to accumulate potential energy, and then suddenly spend it in free action. The storage of energy is then the prime essential. But whereas the sun separates the atoms of oxygen and carbon, another star might put forth other chemical elements which would then have to be associated or dissociated by entirely different physical means. The result would be living forms totally unlike any we know, with different anatomy and different physiology. Yet the sensori-motor function would be preserved. Different as the forms might be from any we can imagine, they would yet be living forms : they would be capable of catching up usable energy and expending it in explosive actions, as is the business of life. On each planet of each solar system, as it does on this earth, life would choose the fittest means to obtain its end in the circumstances with which it was confronted. So it was that Bergson came to the conclusion that life is possible, "probably, in all the worlds suspended from all the stars."

So what, when I wrote it in 1896, was hardly more than a speculation has become, in 1936, a probability amounting to a reasonable certainty. It is at least a high probability that intelligent beings exist in many other parts of the universe than on this planet alone—and that some of them may be higher than ourselves.

In what outward form they may be cast we cannot, of course, form the slightest conception. A visit to the Zoological Gardens or a Natural History Museum shows the extraordinary variety of life there is on this planet. There we see some accustomed to live in the water, some on dry land, some burrowing in the earth, some flying in the air, animals varying from elephants to mice, birds from albatrosses to humming-birds, fishes from sharks to angel-fishes, insects from butterflies to fleas, besides all the host of slugs, snails, and such-like molluscs. Marvellous is the variety and richness of life on this planet. It is not hard, therefore, to suppose that under very different conditions from any here life may have assumed on other planets forms of which it is quite impossible for us to conceive. But if we cannot conceive their outward form we may, on the principle of the connexity of things, have a shrewd idea of their inward spirit. We may take our highest spiritual experiences and assume them as indicative of the essential nature of the universe, and on this assumption we may conjecture that the higher beings on other planets would manifest the common universal spirit in a higher degree. A slug would find it hard to conceive of life on the scale of King George's Silver Jubilee celebrations. And we would also be in difficulty when trying to conceive the spiritual life of these higher stellar beings. But we would not be in such difficulties as the slug. For rare men in rare moments—holy men of the Himalaya among them—have had inklings of that state of life. We call it the Kingdom of Heaven. And we have good reason for supposing that it does actually exist at the present time on some planet of some star.

Far more important, however, than these conjectures as to the existence of living beings on other planets, and a preliminary necessity, is a consideration of the fundamental nature of this world in which we find ourselves. And when we are alone among the mountains we are especially disposed to think of this. We want to know what the world really is at bottom. We would have as true a conception as possible of this universe with which we are so inextricably bound up.

Remote from the distractions of common life, impressed by the immensities about us, by the magnitude of the mountains, the utter purity of their summits, and the mellow radiance of the stars, we ponder deeply on all we have read or heard about the inner nature and constitution of things—what is the Motive Power of the universe, what it is that ultimately drives the world, and what it is driving at. In the old days it was believed that a Supreme Being, dwelling in the skies, far apart from men, created this earth and the sun and stars, and the plants and animals and us men, and from there looked down upon His handiwork. When the flaws in this conception of things became apparent, a precisely opposite view came into fashion. There was no need to conceive of a God at all, it was thought. All took place in accordance with certain physical and chemical laws. By a happy chance, a fortuitous concourse of atoms one day produced life on this planet. Then, life once produced, a struggle between living things began. The fittest survived. As a result, higher and higher beings came into existence, and so we had the world as we see it to-day. But in the course of time—though a very long time—this sun will cool down, life on this planet will become impossible. Similarly, all other suns will cool down, and any life there may be on the planets of other suns will disappear also. Nothing will be left of life—or even of matter—but a dead level of ineffectual energy. So runs this theory.

An alternative to this melancholy view of things is the conception of the universe as ultimately spiritual—what we see with our eyes and touch with our hands being but the outward, visible, tangible aspect of an inner Mind or Spirit or Personality or Supra-Personality. And this is the view which most mountaineers would probably come to accept as they meditated on it in the mountains themselves. When we see or touch a man's body we know that what we actually see and touch is not the real thing about the man—not the thing about a man which matters most. We know that behind what we see and touch is the real man—the man who thinks and feels and acts. Behind the outward aspect of the man is the personality of the man. And so, according to this view, is it with the universe. Behind the outward aspect of the universe is the Personality of the universe. And, in this case, a single individual would bear to the universe, as a whole, much the same relationship as a germ-cell in my body bears to me. That germ-cell is stamped in the image of me, for it is capable in the growing babe, and infant, and man, of reproducing all my main characteristics. I am working in and through it, though above it and beyond, and far greater than it. And so it is, on this theory, with an individual man in relation to the universe as a whole. He is stamped in the image of the " I " of the universe. This " I," or Personality, or Supra-Personality, or Creative Spirit of the Universe, or God—by whichever style we may wish to term this It or Him—is working in and through as well as high above him, and is as far greater than him as he is than the germ-cell.

The main characteristics of this Supra-Personality we would gather from a study of the most perfect of Its products known to us. The most perfect product we know of upon this planet we men think are men. We, more fully and richly than the highest animals, or the most fascinating birds, manifest the true nature of the Spirit that impels the universe. Hindus look upon Krishna as the highest being who has appeared upon earth, Buddhists upon Buddha, Christians upon Christ, Muslims upon Mahomed. They may differ in their opinion, but all have an ideally perfect man in view, working for an ideally perfect community. And that ideal of perfection does represent as nearly as we imperfect men can approximate to it the nature of that Supra-Personality which is unceasingly at work behind the outward aspect of the universe, including us men, and working with an energy to which no limit can be assigned, and with a power of creating and loving which surpasses all we can imagine.

So when we feel ourselves yearning after that ideal perfection—after the most complete truth, the most perfect beauty, or the sublimest good, or all combined in utter holiness—we are, in fact, experiencing the working in us of the Supra-Personality. And if we should want to be strengthened in our endeavours to attain that perfection, our obvious course would be to open the windows of our soul to the inflow of Its influence and let it blow through us to the most hidden interstices of our being. In other words, to pray and meditate. One person will dash through the Alps in a motor car, merely giving a hasty glance at the beauty around him. Another will sit for hours on the mountain-side contemplating all the beauties, noting exactly what constituted each beauty, meditating intently upon it, absorbing it into his being, making it a part of himself for the rest of his life, and deriving an exquisite enjoyment from this intensity of activity. And it is obviously this latter—this pilgrim mountaineer—who will get nearer to knowing the ultimate nature of the Spirit which is driving the whole world-process, and who will imbibe most of that Spirit to carry him through the necessary work of the world.

At this point, however, the congenital pessimist will argue that this is very well for a time, but as the body dies so will the universe die. Even if we achieve our most cherished ambitions they will vanish in the end, he will say. But there is no need for the less pessimistically inclined of us to accept his conclusions. We have just shown that there are perfectly legitimate grounds for holding that the universe, like ourselves, is ultimately spiritual. That maintained co-ordination of parts which we call life may be inherent in what we are disposed to look upon as lifeless matter. As we come to know an atom better, it may be as truly conceived of as spiritual as material. The whole universe may be alive—may be a living universe and a spiritual universe. There is ample justification for holding such a view. And, as we have already seen, many of the most eminent philosophers and scientists of the day hold it.

It may be admitted that owing to the cooling of the sun, life may disappear from this planet. But while it may be disappearing here it may be gradually appearing on the planet of some other sun. If, as there are good grounds for believing, the universe is ultimately spiritual, and if spiritual laws, not the laws of physics and chemistry, in the end prevail, then Spirit will be at work always and everywhere in the universe, fashioning new forms of life out of the "matter" of the universe. And the process may not be cyclical, wheel-like, with the same point coming round and round again. It may be rhythmical, as we see on this planet when we note the wheat sprouting in one part at the very time when it is being harvested at another. The world-process driven by Spirit may be an everlastingly rhythmic process. Just as life may be dying away in one part of the universe it may be reaching the acme of perfection in another. And as all parts of the universe are most intimately connected with all other parts, and Spirit with matter, the drive to perfection in the waxing planet may have come in part from the expiring life in the waning planet. And, on this view, whatever may happen to a body or a planet, the Spirit will never die. Every good deed, every creation of beauty, every effort after perfection, will work on everlastingly. And knowing this we may rejoice in our doing.

We will not blind ourselves to the evil in the world. We are aware of the suffering all about us. But men must instinctively feel that life is good on the whole, or they would not cling to it as they do—cling to it with the tenacity they show in the case of shipwrecks, or in times of famine. Pain, real and cruel though it undoubtedly is, experience constantly shows us is alleviated in the passage of time—in other words, by the slow soothing of the world-process. Evil also is redeemed in the long-run by that same silent, mitigating process. All this points to the conclusion that the inexhaustible energy at work in the world is working on the whole, and in the final process of things, for good. Pain is being transmuted into joy, and evil redeemed by good. Evil is real but transient, while no good is ever wasted. Evil is the negative: good the positive. So looking at things in the long length of days it is the good and not the evil which gains the upper hand. The higher self wins through in its struggle with the lower.

This does not mean that men need not trouble themselves to fight against evil. It is only through men that evil is overcome—evil in themselves and in others. But it does mean that in striving for the good men may feel that they have the whole impetus of the universe behind them. In struggling to climb a mountain the climber has the force of gravity perpetually dragging him downward. But he has that within him strong enough to prevail against it, and he gains the summit. So is it in man's struggle against evil. Evil is as real as the force of gravity. But man has in him what will overcome it. In the end it is the good which prevails.

What all this will signify for the pilgrim in his Mountain Sanctuary is that now he can find leisure to spend a few nights in the open with the stars as well as with the mountains, and so make himself at home in the universe at large as well as on this planet, he will be able to see things in their due proportion, size them up at their true worth, and so see himself in his true cosmic setting.

The first immediate and overwhelming impression which will be produced upon him as he contemplates stars and mountains together will be one of awe and wonder. Then, as he comes to meditate silently upon this cosmic setting in which he now finds himself, and to think things out to their last analysis, he will scarcely come to any other conclusion than that the mountains and the stars are but the outward manifestation of that same Divine Personality which is welling up within himself when he is aspiring to be as pure and lofty as the mountains, and as calm and steadfast as the stars.

Science has always assumed the intelligibility of the universe. It has proceeded on the assumption that the world is not ultimately governed by pure chance. And now the pilgrim will probably find that, behind the working of the world-process which is ever proceeding around him and in him, as Ground of all things, is the Intelligence of a great Mathematician, the sense of Order, Method, and Discipline of a great Governor, the feeling for Form and Colour of a great Artist, the exceeding lovingkindness of a great Lover, the prophetic Solicitude of a great Mother—all bound together in some unifying Personality, and yet transcended in that which is beyond any Personality of which he can in any way conceive.

And as he feels the stars and mountains drawing his

soul out to its farthest stretch, he will find himself at the same time absorbing more and more of their essential spirit. Then, perchance, a day may come to one in ten thousand pilgrims when the barriers of the self will seem to melt away and the overflowing flood-stream of the world come racing through him. Well-nigh overpowered will he be by the Spirit of the Universe, thus coursing so irresistibly through him ; and scarce able will he be to contain himself. Yet never will he feel more truly, fully, and intensely himself. His whole soul will be satisfied. He will have discovered the secret of the world. He will be convinced past all refutation of the goodness in the heart of the world, and therefore of every human being.

And because of this white-heat of exaltation he will be fired with a consuming love of the world. What he has now experienced he would have all others share with him. He would lift the whole world to where he had himself been exalted. And he will feel himself of an inexhaustible vitality—strong to accomplish his end. Faith to remove mountains of Himalayan magnitude will possess him. Through mountains of doubt and depression and persistent obstruction the rays of his joy will unerringly pierce. Before them the greatest obstructions will dissolve as mists at sunrise. Creative power, too, will be his. As the entire universe has conspired to produce him, so will he conspire with the universe to bring into being the more radiant world of the future. And of this the intensest star at the zenith will stand for ever as the shining symbol.

INDEX

INDEX

PRINTED IN GREAT BRITAIN AT
THE PRESS OF THE PUBLISHERS

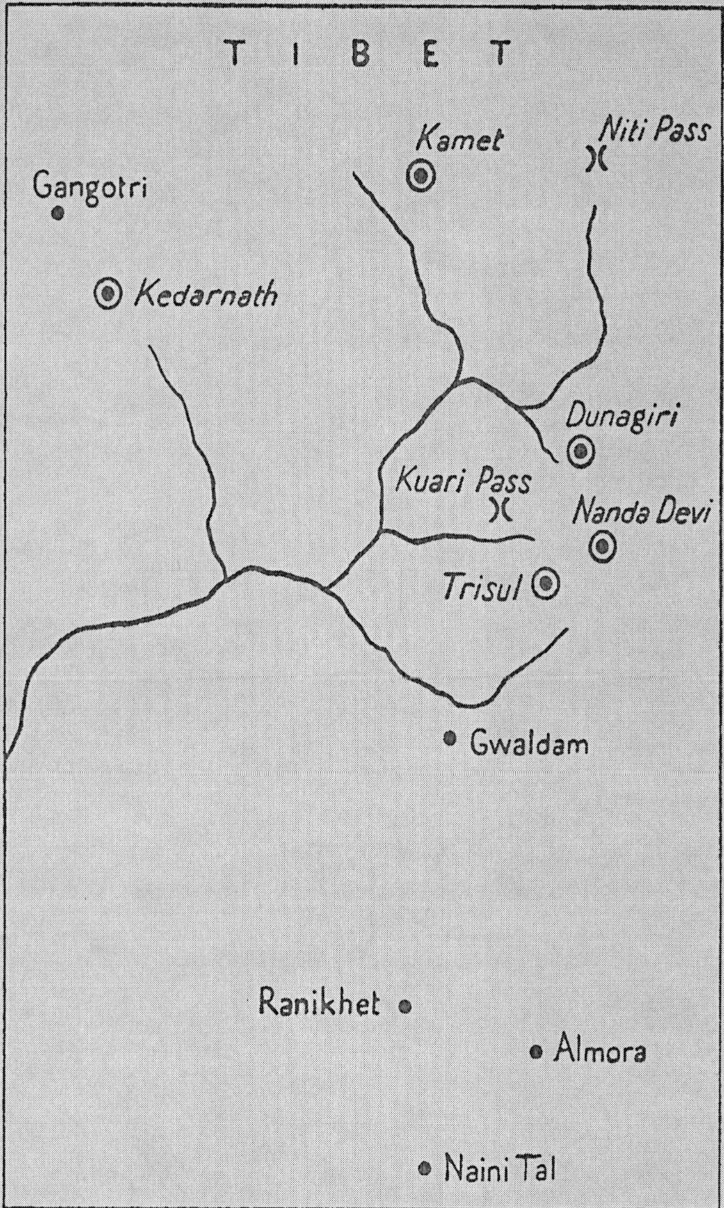

The Kumaon Himalaya.

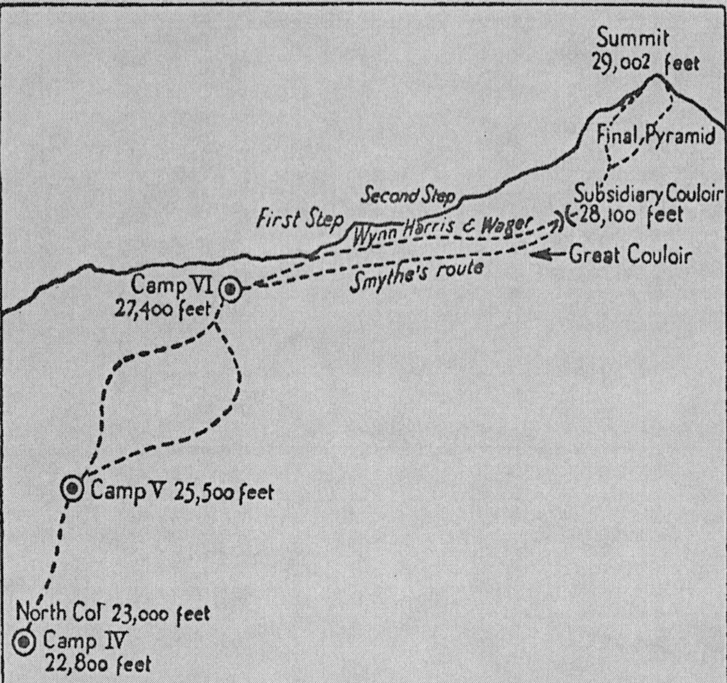

Diagram of North Face *of* Everest *showing* Camps *and* routes *taken by* climbers *in* 1933

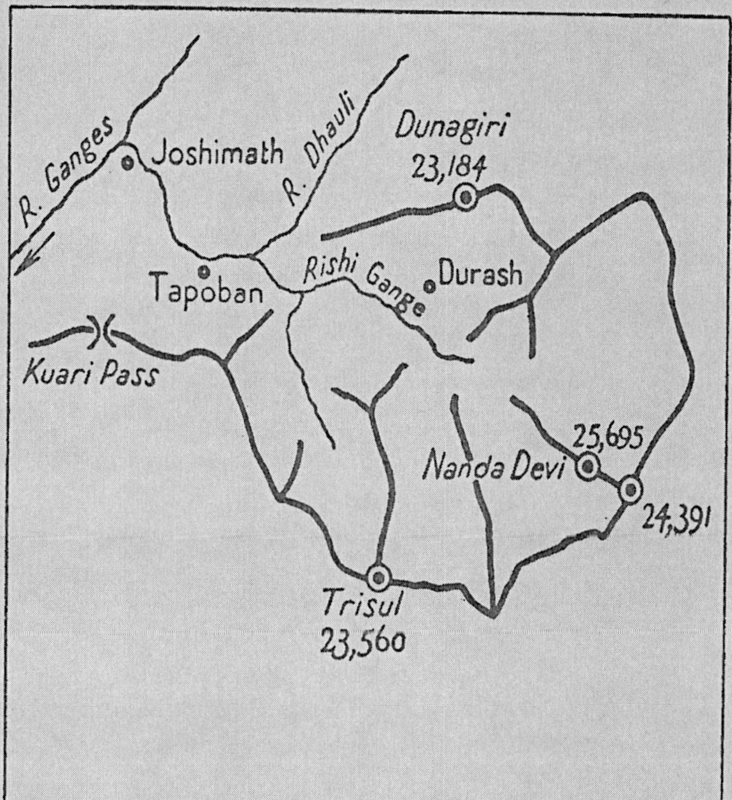

Nanda Devi and Trisul.